D1074830

Social Work and the Law

Proceedings of the National Organization of Forensic Social Work, 2000

Pre-publication REVIEWS, COMMENTARIES, EVALUATIONS . . .

"This introductory work is very easy to read and goes a long way toward finally answering the frequently asked question 'What is forensic social work?'

Progressive social work programs and clinicians determined to widen the standard vision of social work should benefit from the range of issues presented by the contributors. *Social Work and the Law* would also serve as a valuable primer for social work students interested in pursuing forensic social work but not familiar with opportunities for practice in this field.

This book may be the one tool needed to emphasize how beneficial forensic social workers can be to the judicial system. The timing couldn't be better!"

Shelli Schade, LMSW, DAPA
Director of Social Services,
Medical Center at Terrell, TX

"*Social Work and the Law* provides readers with varied and useful content. The chapters on stalking and the links between animal abuse, child abuse, and domestic violence are refreshingly new and thought-provoking. The chapter on multidisciplinary life history research in forensic social work is thorough and informative. The chapter on psychological testing should be a must-read for social workers who tend to leave 'that testing stuff' to psychologists. The emerging specialty of forensic social work should benefit greatly from this book and what it offers."

Raymond J. Olszewski, Jr., LMSW
Forensic Evaluator and Trainer,
Assessment and Resource Center,
Columbia, SC

More pre-publication
REVIEWS, COMMENTARIES, EVALUATIONS . . .

"*Social Work and the Law* is a convenient source for obtaining a snapshot of the current issues in the field. It offers comprehensive, balanced coverage of legal, theoretical, and 'practical' concerns of anyone interested in the marriage between forensic science and other social sciences. This book, especially the chapters regarding links among animal abuse, child abuse, and domestic violence, using multidisciplinary life history research in forensic social work, and psychological testing for social workers in a forensic setting, provides an integrative multidisciplinary look at how and why humans behave as they do—with an emphasis on the complementary approach of forensic psychology. This compilation of papers could be of great value and prove useful to students and teachers alike."

Lynyonne Cotton, PhD
Assistant Professor of Psychology,
St. Mary's College of California

"*Social Work and the Law* is a wonderful introductory book for students and professionals in social work looking for a solid representation of legal issues relevant to the field. The broad perspective of this book incorporates the importance of law in social work curricula development, policy, advocacy, and clinical intervention in a variety of social work settings. The range of social work issues addressed is critical to understanding the integration of law in the social work profession.

Every student needs to read this informative book. I found the section on competency to stand trial, stalking, the use of multidisciplinary life stories, and psychological testing to be of great value and ideal for helping students contextualize legal aspects they will encounter as professionals. This text clearly provides an illustration of some basic legal concerns that have serious implications for the delivery of social work services."

Claudia Lawrence-Webb, DSW, MSW
Assistant Professor,
University of Maryland,
Baltimore County

"*Social Work and the Law* paints an instructive picture of the practice of social work within a diverse group of legal settings. As the reader moves through chapters on curriculum development, drug courts, and other areas of disciplinary interface, it becomes apparent that many of the essential elements of forensic social work are included therein.

This text organizes the basic social work functions of assessment treatment, advocacy, and research into a cogent analysis of their relationships with legal issues. Criminal and civil perspectives are discussed. The chapters on multidisciplinary approaches and psychological testing reflect the importance of teamwork in forensic social work. Traditional forensic practice has required the use of work product from multiple disciplines. The book emphasizes this need in its presentation of life history research. This book can serve as an important primer for those contemplating a future in the practice and instruction of forensic social work."

Edward L. Garner, PhD
Clinic Supervisor,
San Bernardino County Department
of Behavioral Health, CA

More pre-publication
REVIEWS, COMMENTARIES, EVALUATIONS . . .

"*Social Work and the Law* provides informative, enlightening reports from various views in an overall very readable and readily applicable format. The proceedings cover a wide range of topics that are relevant to numerous settings for social workers, whatever their forensic experience and/or expertise. As a forensic social worker responsible for discharging forensic clients suffering from chronic mental illnesses, I found this book informative regarding process, insightful regarding clinical issues, and instructive regarding court preparation."

Peggy Reed-Lohmeyer, MSW, LCSW
Clinical Social Worker
and Team Leader,
Fulton State Hospital, MO

The Haworth Press®
New York • London • Oxford

NOTES FOR PROFESSIONAL LIBRARIANS AND LIBRARY USERS

This is an original book title published by The Haworth Press, Inc. Unless otherwise noted in specific chapters with attribution, materials in this book have not been previously published elsewhere in any format or language.

CONSERVATION AND PRESERVATION NOTES

All books published by The Haworth Press, Inc. and its imprints are printed on certified pH neutral, acid free book grade paper. This paper meets the minimum requirements of American National Standard for Information Sciences-Permanence of Paper for Printed Material, ANSI Z39.48-1984.

Social Work and the Law

Proceedings of the National Organization of Forensic Social Work, 2000

THE HAWORTH PRESS
New, Recent, and Forthcoming Titles
of Related Interest

Forensic Social Work: Legal Aspects of Professional Practice, Second Edition by Robert L. Barker and Douglas M. Branson

The Witness Stand: A Guide for Clinical Social Workers in the Courtroom by Janet Vogelsang

Social Work Ethics on the Line by Charles S. Levy

Families and Law edited by Lisa J. McIntyre and Marvin B. Sussman

Social Work Practice in the Military edited by James G. Daley

Sexual Abuse Litigation: A Practical Resource for Attorneys, Clinicians, and Advocates edited by Rebecca A. Rix

Protecting Judgment-Impaired Adults: Issues, Interventions, and Policies edited by Edmund F. Dejowski

Child Custody: Legal Decisions and Family Outcomes edited by Craig A. Everett

Counseling Juvenile Offenders in Institutional Settings edited by Sol Chaneles

We Are Not Alone: A Guidebook for Helping Professionals and Parents Supporting Adolescent Victims of Sexual Abuse by Jade Christine Angelica

We Are Not Alone: A Teenage Girl's Personal Account of Incest from Disclosure Through Prosecution and Treatment by Jade Christine Angelica

We Are Not Alone: A Teenage Boy's Personal Account of Child Sexual Abuse from Disclosure Through Prosecution and Treatment by Jade Christine Angelica

Social Work and the Law

Proceedings of the National Organization of Forensic Social Work, 2000

Ira A. Neighbors
Anne Chambers
Ellen Levin
Gila Nordman
Cynthia Tutrone
Editors

The Haworth Press®
New York • London • Oxford

The Haworth Press, Inc., 10 Alice Street, Binghamton, NY 13904-1580.

Cover design by Jennifer M. Gaska.

Library of Congress Cataloging-in-Publication Data

Social work and the law : proceedings of the National Organization of Forensic Social Work, 2000 / Ira Neighbors, editors . . . [et al.].
p. cm.
Includes bibliographical references and index.
ISBN 0-7890-1547-1 (alk. paper)—ISBN 0-7890-1548-X (alk. paper)
1. Forensic sociology—United States—Congresses. 2. Social workers—Legal status, laws, etc.—United States—Congresses. I. Neighbors, Ira. II. National Organization of Forensic Social Work.

KF8968.7.A75 S63 2002
361.3'2'0973—dc21

2001051592

CONTENTS

ABOUT THE EDITORS

Ira A. Neighbors, DSW, BCD, LCSW, is President of the National Organization of Forensic Social Work. He is visiting as Associate Professor in the School of Social Work at Southern University in New Orleans to assist in the development of a forensic social work program. He has developed a class in the specialty area of forensic social work at California State University in San Bernardino, and is a faculty member of Tulane University's School of Social Work Center for Life-Long Learning, Post-MSW Certificate Program in Forensic Social Work.

Anne Chambers, MSW, LCSW, is past President of the National Organization of Forensic Social Work. She is a social work supervisor at the Guhleman Forensic Center of Fulton State Hospital in Fulton, MO.

Ellen Levin, DSW, LCSW-C, AFSW, is President of the Academy of the National Organization of Forensic Social Work. Dr. Levin has more than ten years' experience providing forensic social work services to children, adolescents, and their families. She conducts family assessments, drug and alcohol assessments, and juvenile sex offender program evaluations for the Juvenile Court of Montgomery County in Maryland.

Gila Nordman, AFSW, BCD, LCSW-C, is a Councilor on the board of the National Organization of Forensic Social Work. She is a forensic social worker with CAFÉS—the Child and Adolescent Forensic Evaluation Service—where her responsibilities include completing court-ordered evaluations of individuals and families involved with the Department of Juvenile Justice and the Department of Health and Human Services, as well as the juvenile court. She has more than thirty years of experience as a clinical social worker.

Cynthia Tutrone, LCSW, MSW, is a Councilor on the board of the National Organization of Forensic Social Work and the editor of the NOFSW Newsletter. She is a Protective Services Social Worker Supervisor for the State of Connecticut Department of Children and Families. Ms. Tutrone has also served as Coordinator of the Reducing Inappropriate Sexual Conduct (RISP) program at the Child Guidance Clinic of Southeastern Connecticut and as Program Director for the Center of Adolescent Resources in Massachusetts.

CONTRIBUTORS

Barbara W. Boat, PhD, is Associate Professor, Department of Psychiatry, University of Cincinnati Medical Center, and Executive Director of The Childhood Trust at Children's Hospital Medical Center, Cincinnati. She has conducted research on the use of anatomical dolls in sexual abuse investigations and currently studies relationships among violence to children and animals and domestic violence. Her clinical interests include dissociative disorders and families in which children have experienced domestic violence.

Nina S. Broyles, LCSW, ACSW, JD, is in private practice in clinical and forensic social work. She received a master's degree in social welfare from the University of Southern Mississippi and the Juris Doctorate from Southern University School of Law. She is a member of the Louisiana State Bar Association and several social work organizations.

Guay Chatfield, PhD, is Director of the Office of Court Evaluation in Bridgeport, Connecticut. She has a master's degree in social work from Southern Connecticut State University and a PhD from Fordham University. Her dissertation was entitled "Repeat Competence to Stand Trial Evaluations: A Marker of Severe and Persistent Mental Illness." She is an adjunct faculty member at Southern Connecticut State University.

Shayna Gothard, PhD, is a licensed clinical psychologist who works extensively in the forensic arena. She is in private practice in San Diego, California, where she primarily conducts forensic and clinical evaluations. In addition to her private practice, Dr. Gothard is a consulting psychologist for the San Diego County Forensic Evaluation Unit and a Professor at National University. Dr. Gothard also works as Outcomes Coordinator for Children's Hospital, Center for Child Protection, San Diego. She frequently testifies as an expert witness and is an expert in the areas of malingering, stalking, and mental health outcomes. Dr. Gothard has published in many peer-reviewed journals, including the *American Journal of Psychiatry, Law and Human Behavior,* and *Child Abuse and Neglect: The International Journal.* In addition, she is a frequent conference presenter.

Lyndia Green-Faust, JD, MSW, is Assistant Professor in the School of Social Work at Southern University at New Orleans. Prior to joining the social work faculty, she taught for nearly twenty years in the Criminal Justice Department. She received her MSW from the University of Louisville, Kent School of Social Work, and her Juris Doctorate from the Rutgers University School of Law. She is a member of the Louisiana State Bar Association, and she holds memberships in several law and social work organizations.

Cecile C. Guin, PhD, LCSW, ACSW, is the Director of the Louisiana State University School of Social Work, Office of Social Service Research and Development. She received her PhD in social work from the University of Texas-Arlington, and an MSW from Louisiana State University. She has many publications and presentations, as well as professional affiliations and appointments.

Katie Heffernan, LCSW, is a social worker in the Office of Public Defender Services, Psychiatric Defense Unit, Bridgeport, Connecticut. She has a master's degree in social work from Southern Connecticut State University. Her thesis focused on "Perceptions of Mental Health Providers Regarding Predicting Violence of Mentally Ill Offenders."

Kim McKeon, LCSW, is a social worker in the Office of the Public Defender Services, Psychiatric Defense Unit, Bridgeport, Connecticut. She has a master's degree in social work from the University of Connecticut School of Social Work. She is an adjunct faculty member at local community colleges.

Thomas S. Merrill, PhD, is Director of Psychological Service at Our Lady of the Lake Regional Center in Baton Rouge. He received his PhD from the University of Texas at Austin. He has received numerous awards and is a member of various psychological associations. In addition, he has conducted a variety of research, has made presentations, and has had papers published.

Jacquelyn Mitchell, JD, LCISW, is a member of the graduate faculty of the Jackson State University School of Social Work. She writes and presents regularly on the areas of social work and the American legal system, mediation, social work ethics, diversity, policy, and macro practice. A social worker and attorney, she holds membership and leadership positions in social work and legal organizations. Dr. Mitchell regularly serves as a member of the faculty for National Organization of Forensic Social Workers annual conferences.

Julie Schroeder, PhD, received an MSW from the University of Illinois, Urbana-Champaign, and a PhD in social work from Tulane University. She is Assistant Professor at the Louisiana State University Graduate School of Social Work. She is also a member of the LSU Office of Social Research and Development research team, which recently completed a statewide implementation evaluation of the Louisiana drug courts.

Angela Trainham, LCSW, received a bachelor's degree in counseling from Holy Cross College in New Orleans and a master's degree in social work from Southern University at New Orleans. She has worked in criminal justice for twenty years with adults and juveniles and helped design and was Director of the Jefferson Parish (Louisiana) Juvenile Justice and Delinquency Prevention. She has monitored and evaluated drug court implementation and treatment in multiple sites for the Louisiana State University School of Social Work, and the Office of Social Service Research and Development. She has conducted numerous workshops on the risks and protective factors, and the treatment needs of juvenile offenders.

Karen van Beyer, PhD, LCSW, is a faculty member of the Tulane University Department of Psychiatry and School of Social Work. She received her PhD in Sociology and an MSW at Tulane University. She is the secretary of the National Organization of Forensic Social Work (2000-2001). She also has a private practice and holds memberships in several professional social work organizations.

Foreword

Within the field of social work, there has been a rapid expansion of the issues relative to the area of forensic social work. Forensic social work is the interface of social work with questions and issues relating to the law and the legal system. A forensic social worker must call upon specialized knowledge obtained from principles and practices within the field, familiarity with the law and the legal system, and careful evaluations of clients and situations. The forensic social worker may be called upon to provide a variety of services, including consultation, education, and training to a variety of personnel in the legal arena, including persons involved in civil, criminal, and juvenile justice, law enforcement, legislation, as well as attorneys and members of the public. Forensic social workers may provide diagnosis, treatment, and recommendations on issues such as adult and child mental status, interests, capabilities, and ability to testify, and may serve as expert witnesses on many issues involving the interaction between social work and the legal system. In most, if not all, of these areas, there is a growing body of jurisprudence that recognizes social workers, particularly forensic and/or clinical social workers, as expert witnesses. Social workers who have not had training or education that includes familiarity with the adversary system or the issues that civil and criminal justice systems face will find themselves at a disadvantage. Having been a social worker, lawyer, and a judge for twenty-eight years with degrees and experience in both law and social work, I have seen the increasing demand for legal knowledge in the social work arena. Social workers must acquaint themselves with their role in the legal system. This book contains a compilation of articles that discuss some of the many topics relevant to today's social worker. The reader should be able to gain insight into some of the issues intrinsic to the practice of forensic social work in today's society.

Judge Sol Gothard, JD, MSW, ACSW

Preface

"Social Work and the Law" was the title of the conference of the National Organization of Forensic Social Work (NOFSW) held in Palm Springs, California, in May 2000. Each chapter in this publication was presented as a paper at the conference. The NOFSW conference has been conducted for nearly twenty years to showcase some of the cutting-edge thinking in forensic social work, which has been identified as a new specialty area of professional social work practice.

The chapters are presented close to their original form to recreate the spirit of the conference. However, the authors have also updated their work to include more recent references. Judge Sol Gothard introduces this publication by expounding upon the many issues forensic social workers are confronted with in today's society. The chapter by Ira A. Neighbors, Lyndia Green-Faust, and Karen van Beyer sets the stage by bringing to the fore the curricula development in master's in social work (MSW) and post-MSW programs. Next, Guay Chatfield, Katie Heffernan, and Kim McKeon review their eleven-year case study on competence to stand trial. Shayna Gothard looks at the current science of "stalking." Barbara Boat then takes on another dimension of forensic social work in linking animal abuse/child abuse to psychological and legal ramifications. Julie Schroeder and Angela Trainham reveal how drug courts are empowered through evaluations. Jacquelyn Mitchell presents yet another aspect of forensic social work in posing the question: "Is Social Work Y2K Compliant"? Then, Cecile Guin and Thomas Merrill report on another area of forensic social work by relating how to use multidisciplinary life history research in "Life or Death" sentencing. Nina Broyles encapsulates the proceedings with a chapter on ways to increase the psychomeasurement IQ in legal matters.

Ira A. Neighbors

Chapter 1

Curricula Development in Forensic Social Work at the MSW and Post-MSW Levels

Ira A. Neighbors
Lyndia Green-Faust
Karen van Beyer

This chapter is a by-product of a presentation given at the National Organization of Forensic Social Work (NOFSW) Palm Springs Conference Year 2000. The three presenters are affiliated with the Tulane University School of Social Work and Southern University School of Social Work at New Orleans Graduate School of Social Work. The idea of the presentation was derived from a national survey of graduate schools of social work. One concern of the survey was to find out what schools were doing with regard to forensic social work. Another concern of the survey was to find out if schools of social work make a distinction between forensic social work and social work and the law. This chapter will show the results of the national survey of MSW schools, and the developments taking place in forensic social work in Southern University's MSW curriculum, as well as Tulane University's post-MSW curriculum.

Forensic social work has its origins at the turn of the twentieth century when the social work profession came into existence and was associated with the organization known as the National Conference of Charities and Corrections (Barker and Branson, 2000; Roberts and Brownell, 1999). More and more, the term "forensic social work" is coming into use. Today, forensic social work is seen as a specialty area in social work that links professional social workers to legal matters. Forensic social work suggests that social workers are familiar with laws governing the social work profession and that social workers interface with judges, lawyers, and various other personnel in the legal systems (Barker, 1999).

Social workers are called upon to function effectively in the legal system. Social workers must be knowledgeable about the laws and legal terms that have an impact on the legal and social work professions. It is projected that throughout the twenty-first century, social workers will advocate for clients who have legal problems and/or are involved in the judicial system. Because of the many legal matters confronting social workers, graduate schools of social work should provide training to help meet these needs.

A NATIONAL SURVEY OF SCHOOLS OF SOCIAL WORK

Some questions used to guide NOFSW's 1998 survey of MSW schools of social work are listed as follows: Are graduate schools of social work providing students adequate training to function effectively in the legal world? Is forensic social work another matter (i.e., is there a major difference between the concepts "forensic social work" and "social work and the law")? Often the terms "forensic social work" and "social work and the law" are used interchangeably, which can cause confusion. In attempting to find out the status of forensic social work and social work and the law in graduate schools of social work, a survey was launched by the NOFSW and supported in part by the National Council on Juvenile Court Judges in 1998 (Neighbors, 2000b). The following ten questions were asked of graduate program directors:

1. Does your graduate school of social work/welfare offer a joint MSW/JD degree?
2. Does your graduate school currently offer a course on social work and the law?

3. Does your graduate school offer a class titled "Forensic Social Work?"
4. Does your graduate school offer a forensic social work sequence/track?
5. Does your internship program include placement in forensic settings?
6. Do the MSW students request social work and the law classes?
7. Do the MSW students request forensic social work classes?
8. What are the titles of courses you offer on the topic of social work and the law or forensic social work?
9. Are you contemplating expanding your program to include forensic social work?
10. Are there comments you would like to make?

In total, 122 surveys were sent to MSW programs accredited by the Council on Social Work Education (CSWE). Of the 122 surveys, 72 schools responded which represented a 59 percent return rate. A description of the responding MSW programs, the number and percentages of responses, and the results of the survey are shown in Tables 1.1 through 1.10. The Pearson's r was used to obtain any significant correlation ($p < 05$).

In summary, analyses of the data do not indicate any major surprises, but a few minor ones do surface. It is important to note that the nature of the measure severely limits the ability to perform inferential analyses on the data. Most interesting, in light of one intent of the measure (to internally validate items by way of repetition)—the respondents had a tendency to respond differentially. Despite the letter of introduction stating that the terms "Forensic Social Work" (FSW) and "Social Work and the Law" (SWL) were essentially interchangeable terms for the purposes of the study, respondents seemed to treat the items as separate issues. For example, while 64.3 percent stated that classes in SWL were offered, only 4.3 percent stated that FSW classes were offered.

In addition, there was a significant correlation between students requesting SWL courses and the offering of those courses. Likewise, there was a significant correlation between the students'

TABLE 1.1. Public versus Private

Type of School	Number	%
Public	53	75.7
Private	17	24.3
Total	70	100.0

TABLE 1.2. Joint MSW/JD Degrees

	Number	%
Yes	24	34.3
No	46	65.7
Total	70	100.0

TABLE 1.3. Offer Social Work and Law

	Number	%
Yes	45	64.3
No	25	35.7
Total	70	100.0

TABLE 1.4. Offer Forensic Social Work Class

	Number	%
Yes	3	4.3
No	66	94.3
No Answer	1	1.4
Total	70	100.0

TABLE 1.5. Offer Forensic Social Work Track

	Number	%
Yes	3	4.3
No	66	94.3
No Answer	1	1.4
Total	70	100.0

TABLE 1.6. Forensic Intern Placement

	Number	%
Yes	48	68.6
No	19	27.1
No Answer	3	4.3
Total	70	100.0

TABLE 1.7. Students Requesting Social Work and Law Classes

	Number	%
Yes	49	70.0
No	18	25.7
No Answer	3	4.3
Total	70	100.0

TABLE 1.8. Students Requesting Forensic Social Work Classes

	Number	%
Yes	13	18.6
No	54	77.1
No Answer	3	4.3
Total	70	100.0

TABLE 1.9. Title of Course: Forensic Social Work and the Law

	Number	%
None	29	41.4
FSW/SWL	26	37.2
Special Topics	4	5.7
Multiple Topics	11	15.7
Total	70	100.0

TABLE 1.10. Expanding Program to Include Forensic Social Work

	Number	%
Yes	10	14.3
No	47	67.1
No Answer	11	15.7
Maybe	2	2.9
Total	70	100.0

requests for SWL and FSW offerings in schools. Although from a methodological standpoint this would tend to be problematic, it is possible, despite the introductory letter, that respondents chose to differentiate between the two course titles. One possibility is that the SWL classes are those which focus on the law as it affects the social worker, while the FSW classes emphasize the social worker's role in interacting between the client and the legal system.

No significant correlation between the existence of forensic social work emphasis and field placements in forensic social work settings was shown. However, there was a significant positive correlation between the joint MSW/JD program and FSW field placements. This may be attributable to the fact that only three programs currently offer FSW classes; any significant correlation is unlikely. All three schools that offer FSW classes do offer FSW field placements, but because nearly 70 percent (68.6 percent) of all programs offer FSW placements, any further conclusion would be speculative.

CURRICULUM DEVELOPMENT AT THE MSW LEVEL

In the most simplistic form, forensic social work is defined as social work's interface with the law. The task at hand for the forensic social work committee is to review how forensic social work may become a part of the social work program at Southern University at New Orleans (SUNO). There are pros and cons to merging forensic social work into SUNO's social work curriculum. Four options are provided.

Option I: Infusion

This option would entail including forensic social work in the present course offerings. Under this option, it is believed that forensic social work is already included in the class offerings.

Pro: the pro of this option would be that all students would have exposure to forensic social work in the classes that are presently offered.

Con: this option would require the restructuring or rethinking of the present class curricula to ensure students' exposure to forensic social work.

Option II: Concentration

This option would require the addition of a new concentration consisting of two to three elective classes.

Pro: this option would ensure that students take several classes to expose them to the areas of forensic social work.

Con: there are already three concentrations: Children, youth, and family (CYF), Health/mental health (H/MH), and gerontology (GERON). A fourth option, Forensic social work (FSW), would require additional classes and resources (more students and instructors to teach these classes).

Option III: Certification

This option would entail the addition of several new classes that would focus on students becoming certified in forensic social work. SUNO would award certification to those students completing this option.

Pro: students would be more marketable in the various forensic settings.

Con: similar to a concentration, certification would require additional classes and resources. In addition, being certified by SUNO would not guarantee a student acceptance of the certification by the forensic social work community.

Option IV: Specialization

This option would require students to take the existing classes, but a cohort of students would be provided with specialized forensic social work knowledge in CYF, H/MH, or GERON.

Pro: for a cohort of students (e.g., in CYF), a domestic violence class would include issues in child abuse, elderly abuse, and spousal abuse with special emphasis placed on the various laws affecting these populations.

Con: see Option I: Infusion.

Option V: Continuing Education

This option would allow MSWs to return to weekend/evening/Saturday classes and obtain a certification of completion in forensic social work (see Option III: Certification).

Pro: this option would generate additional funding. Also, with the new licensing laws, alumni would probably be required to obtain continuing education hours. In addition, the money generated would help resolve the resource problem.

Con: previous difficulties in coordinating and administrating weekend/evening/Saturday classes are still problematic.

Resolve

A mixture of Option I and Option II (i.e., Infusion and Concentration) was initiated for the school year 2000-2001. A syllabus for the forensic social work class was developed and implemented (Neighbors, 2000a).

CURRICULUM DEVELOPMENT AT THE POST-MSW LEVEL

Over the Rainbow: The Path to a Forensic Social Work Certificate Program

The title of this section refers to a dream: starting an educational program at the Tulane School of Social Work that would prepare social workers at the master's level for the many areas of practice that interface with the legal system. After working in the forensics division of the Louisiana State University Medical Center (LSUMC)

Department of Psychiatry, for two years, and serving the School of Social Work as a field instructor for ten years, I was disturbed at how poorly students were prepared to practice in areas that require familiarity with basic legal procedures. We seem to let our graduates sink or swim not only to their own detriment, but also to the detriment of their clients.

I envisioned a basic course in forensics that would be part of the general master's level curriculum. I also felt that a forensic track should be offered as an elective within the master's program for those who wanted to specialize in that area. These goals were reified in a proposal that I submitted to the chair of the Educational Policy Committee of Tulane in May of 1997. My path from that beginning in 1997 is the topic of this section. My goal of a course and a track was to be molded and reshaped into a program that fit the needs of the school: In June of 2000, the Tulane School of Social Work began a forensic social work certificate program for post-master's practitioners.

The forces and factors that go into the realization of such a program may be of interest to those who are considering starting a course or program. I would like to map the obstacles and pitfalls that might lie in your path.

Within a school of social work, three structural elements influence the outcome of a proposal for courses in a new area: the university administration, the dean of the school of social work, and the school of social work's curriculum committee. In writing this chapter, Professor Green-Faust, Dr. Neighbors, and I first hypothesized that there would be resistance to change on all three levels. We isolated four types of resistance:

1. Resistance to change in general
2. Academic rivalry
3. Council on Social Work Education (CSWE) requirements
4. Being stuck in a paradigm and failing to read the "signs of the times"

How do we deal with this resistance or how do we "sell" our program at all levels? I will discuss these as I came across them as

I worked toward my dream for forensic social work at my alma mater. Let's look at how or whether these types of resistance operated.

The Curriculum Committee and the General Faculty

My first step was submitting a proposal for a course and/or a track in forensic social work to the curriculum committee. At the time I made my proposal to the committee, the school was undergoing major changes. We had a new dean who had been with the school for two and a half years and a curriculum that had been used in the school for two and a half years. The curriculum had developed in a patchwork manner as the school grew and evolved. This curriculum needed to be reshaped and streamlined. Electives had been added in accord with faculty interests. Therefore, a freeze was put on the development and implementation of new electives. Electives with limited enrollment were dropped.

The structure of the faculty changed drastically when four of the core faculty retired within one year. The faculty reformed without the underlying trust of long-term relationships. A rapid turnover of several faculty members who did not become a part of the new group occurred. The group process went from a relatively brief forming stage to several years of storming.

At about this time, the CSWE requirements became more generalist in nature and more policy oriented. Texts and core curriculum were reformulated to meet the requirements of the CSWE. The curriculum shifted from a "well-known," clinically rich program to one that was more focused on community organization and policy. There was little room for the development of new courses, particularly when each course had to be enriched with new content. On the faculty level, there was controversy over the shift in the focus of the school's vision.

It is no wonder that my proposal was tabled. I was nonetheless asked to serve on the continuing education committee, which was renamed "The Center for Lifelong Learning."

School of Social Work Administration

My next step was to approach the dean. I felt very strongly that the departments of psychiatry and psychology, which had residency training programs and doctoral programs in forensics, were leaving the social work program "in the dust." Yet, as usual, social workers were the primary workers in the "trenches." Both in the jails and in the programs that deal with the socially disadvantaged, social workers provide direct services. Students need to be trained so that they can adequately serve their clients. This is particularly true for new graduates working in agencies that serve low-income groups.

A dual degree in law and social work had been talked about for years but had never been implemented. The deans of both schools were in agreement that such a program should be developed, but it was left up to interested students to work out their own program. (Only one person did so but was not provided with structure by the two schools, so there were many logistical problems in trying to get through the two programs' curricula.)

The dean's response was to ask me to serve on the continuing education committee. The committee that had primarily put on continuing education seminars in the summer, prior to the August deadline for continuing education (CE) credits. Nurtured by the dean's vision of streamlining the master's curriculum and expanding postmaster's education, the CE committee metamorphasized into the Center for Lifelong Learning. The forensic course and track changed into a post-MSW certificate program in forensic social work.

University Administration

In 1998, the university acquired a new president. Our program, as it emerged in its final form, fit in with the new administration's desire to have intrasystemic, collaborative endeavors that would bring the law school, the medical school, and the school of social work together. No resistance to forensic social work was evident on the university level; on the contrary, it fit in with the new president's vision.

On the fiscal administration level, financial constraints mitigate against new programs that do not have a proven ability to pay for themselves or to bring money into the system. The continuing education program emerged as a way of bringing money into the school. It was seen as a multilayered educational system that would allow several points of entry. This was also congruent with the president's perspective.

Thus, in examining the development of forensics at the Tulane School of Social Work, I came to the conclusion that it was the system's context in which the program was proposed that led to the creation of a course for master's level students into a postmaster's, year-long certification program.

REFERENCES

Barker, R. (1999). *The social work dictionary* (Fourth edition). Washington, DC: NASW Press.

Barker, R. and Branson, D.M. (2000). *Forensic social work: Legal aspects of professional practice* (Second edition). Binghamton, NY: The Haworth Press, Inc.

Neighbors, I.A. (2000a). Forensic social work: The interface between social work and the law. In K. van Wormer and A.R. Roberts (Eds.), *Teaching forensic social work: Course outlines on criminal and juvenile justice and victimology* (pp. 113-117). Alexandria, VA: Council on Social Work Education (CSWE), Inc.

Neighbors, I.A. (2000b). Results of the National Organization of Forensic Social Work survey. *Newsletter of NOFSW,* III(8). Ann Arbor, MI: NOFSW.

Roberts, A. and Brownell, P. (1999). A century of forensic social work: Bridging the past to the present. *Social Work,* 44(4): 359-369.

Chapter 2

Competence to Stand Trial: An Eleven-Year Case Study

Guay Chatfield
Katie Heffernan
Kim McKeon

COMPETENCE IN CONNECTICUT

The Connecticut General Statute §54-56d governs competence in Connecticut. The competency statute states that "a defendant shall not be tried, convicted or sentenced while he is not competent" (Competency to Stand Trial, 1995). A defendant is not competent if he or she is unable to understand the proceedings against him or her or is unable to assist in his or her own defense. A §54-56d examination can be ordered at any time during a case, and can be requested by the defense counsel, court, or prosecuting attorney. The examiner may be a private forensic psychiatrist or a forensic team from one of the offices of court evaluations.

Three offices of court evaluations (formally known as the court diagnostic clinics) were established in July 1975 to accommodate changes in Connecticut law decentralizing the forensic evaluation process. Prior to 1975, all evaluations to assess competency to stand trial were performed on an inpatient basis at a state hospital. The Connecticut State Departments of the Judiciary, Probation, and Corrections collaborated to develop the three court diagnostic clinics, which began operation as a three-year demonstration project funded by the Law Enforcement Assistance Administration (LEAA). Upon the expiration of LEAA funding in 1978, the Connecticut Department of Mental Health assumed fiscal responsibility for the Clinic's operation. Presently, the Department of Mental Health (now known as the Department of Mental Health and Addiction Services) continues to assume fiscal responsibility with additional support from Yale University for a fourth clinic (Courts Diagnostic Clinic, 1980).

In Connecticut, licensed clinical social workers are an intricate part of the competency evaluation process. The forensic team also consists of a psychiatrist and a psychologist. The social workers are the team leaders and ultimately responsible for the evaluation.

The examinations take place within the jail setting if the defendant is incarcerated, or at one of the offices of the court evaluations if he or she is out on bond or a promise to appear. Generally, the social worker writes the report; the psychiatrist and psychologist give feedback, and then the "agreed-upon report" is submitted to the court. Although any member of the team may testify according to the statute, the social worker plans his or her schedule to be available for court testimony and is usually the one to testify.

The competency interviews last approximately sixty to ninety minutes. Before each interview, the team reviews the referral materials in the defendant's file. There is an initial interviewer who directs the questioning. The team members rotate in serving as the initial interviewer. The questions address the defendant's understanding of his or her current legal situation and ability to assist in his or her defense. The questions regarding the legal status include the following: the charges, the relevant facts, the legal issues and procedures, the function of court personnel, the mechanics of pleading and plea-bargaining, and the possible dispositions and penalties. The questions in regard to assisting in his or her defense include the ability to: identify and locate witnesses, comprehend instructions and advice, make decisions after receiving advice, maintain a collaborative relationship with attorneys, follow testimony for accuracy, testify and be cross-examined, tolerate stress, and refrain from irrational behavior (Courts Diagnostic Clinic, 1980).

At the competency hearing, the court will read the report, hear the testimony, and make a final determination. If the defendant is found competent to stand trial, he or she faces the original charges in court. If the defendant is found not competent to stand trial, he or she is committed to inpatient treatment for the purpose of restoration to competence. Outpatient treatment in the community is an option for a few defendants who have a proven track record of treatment compliance. The defendant may be committed to the Department of Mental Health and Addiction Service (DMHAS), Department of Mental Retardation (DMR), or Department of Children and Families (DCF) (Competency to Stand Trial, 2000).

The period of commitment for restoration of competency can be any time up to eighteen months. When the treating forensic team believes that the defendant has been restored to competency, a report is submitted to the court. The forensic social worker from the restoration team will go to court and testify regarding the defendant's competency status. If the court finds the defendant competent, the defendant returns to court to face the original criminal charges (Competency to Stand Trial, 2000).

Historically, if the defendants were found not competent and considered by the forensic team not to be restorable, the court would dismiss the charges without the option to order periodic examinations. At that time, it would be up to the agency that has custody of the defendant to move for a civil commitment if appropriate (Competency to Stand Trial, 1998). In 1998, as a result of *State of Connecticut v. Kenneth Curtis,* the statute was amended to include the option of ordering periodic examinations.

STATE OF CONNECTICUT v. KENNETH CURTIS

In 1988, the Stratford, Connecticut, Police Department arrested Kenneth Curtis on the charges of murder, criminal attempt to commit murder, and assault in the first degree. These charges stemmed from allegations that on October 30, 1987, Mr. Curtis struck his ex-fiancée and her friend with his pickup truck, exited his vehicle with a handgun, and shot his ex-fiancée in the head, fatally wounding her. He then shot himself in the head. As a result of the gunshot wound, he was in a coma for six weeks, sustained a traumatic brain injury, and was paralyzed (Stratford Police Arrest Warrant, 1988). Due to his diminished capacity of intellectual functioning, his defense attorney requested a competence to stand trial evaluation.

The forensic team of the Bridgeport Office of Court Evaluation met with Mr. Curtis on three or more occasions over the period of eighteen months. Throughout this period, he had difficulty understanding and answering questions. He had no memory of the events that led to his arrest, and he was not able to adequately discuss any aspects of the case. He was not able to understand the proceedings against him, and was unable to assist in his defense. Therefore, in May 1989, the forensic team concluded that Mr. Curtis was incompetent and could not be restored to competency (*State of Connecticut v. Kenneth Curtis* Competency Evaluation, 1989).

In June 1989, Judge Richard Damiani accepted the forensic team's conclusion. The charges were still pending, but Mr. Curtis was released from custody. Based on the prosecution's request, Judge Damiani ordered that Mr. Curtis be examined every year to determine if his condition had improved. The defense objected, indicating that the law in Connecticut allows only an eighteen-month period for restoration and that the charges must be dropped. DMHAS then had the option to file for a civil commitment. The defense appealed the judge's order and, in June 1990, won in appellate court. According to the state statute, no further evaluation of Mr. Curtis was possible (*State of Connecticut v. Kenneth Curtis,* Decision, 1999).

In 1997, the Stratford Police, acting on information that Kenneth Curtis was attending college, executed a search warrant for Mr. Curtis's academic records. They discovered from these records that since 1992 he had attended three colleges and had maintained a 3.3 grade point average. As a result of this investigation, in November 1997, an arrest warrant was executed for the original charges (Stratford Police Arrest Warrant, 1997).

The defense appealed the rearrest, and in October 1998, lost in the state supreme court. In November 1998, Judge George Thim ordered a competence to stand trial evaluation. The forensic team from the Bridgeport Office of Court Evaluation evaluated

Mr. Curtis for approximately five hours in January 1999. His presentation was identical to that in the original competency evaluation. Although he appeared gravely disabled and incompetent, the team decided to hold off on a decision.

> The Office of Court Evaluations examined Mr. Curtis, reviewed voluminous documents concerning his medical and educational history and interviewed persons who have treated him, taught him and socialized with him. In considering Mr. Curtis's competency, the evaluation team considered his ability to assimilate information, his capacity for abstract reasoning, and his ability to communicate with others. While Mr. Curtis was slow in processing information, the team concluded that this impairment is not of an extent that would render him unable to understand the charges and proceedings, or to be able to participate in his own defense. The team found that Mr. Curtis was able to discuss his charges and the appeal process rationally with various persons, including his psychiatrists, neurologist, and a college instructor. The team concluded that there is a reasonable degree of medical certainty that Mr. Curtis is able to understand the charge against him and participate in his defense. (*State of Connecticut v. Kenneth Curtis,* Competence to Stand Trial Evaluation Report, 1999, p. 27)

As a result of the additional collateral information, the team determined that they had enough evidence to demonstrate that Mr. Curtis had a higher level of functioning than he had presented in his evaluation. In May 1999, the forensic team submitted a report to the court with the opinion that he was competent. Competency hearings then commenced, and in August 1999, Judge George Thim determined that Mr. Curtis was competent to stand trial. In the written decision Judge Thim stated, "It is quite clear to this Court that Kenneth Curtis has purposely exaggerated his symptoms in an effort to influence the outcome of this criminal prosecution" (*State of Connecticut v. Kenneth Curtis*, Decision, 1999, p. 1).

In September 1999, instead of proceeding to a trial, Mr. Curtis pled guilty to manslaughter in the first degree under the Alford Doctrine, in which he does not admit guilt but acknowledges that the state has enough evidence for a likely conviction if the case went to trial (Hanrahan, 1999). In December 1999, Mr. Curtis was sentenced to the maximum penalty of twenty years in jail (Tepfer, 1999).

CONCLUSION

In 1998, as a result of *State of Connecticut v. Kenneth Curtis,* the Office of State's Attorney petitioned the legislature to amend the competency statute subsection (m) to read "If the court orders the release of a defendant charged with the commission of a crime that resulted in the death or serious physical injury . . . of another person, it may, on its own motion or on motion of the prosecuting authority, order, as a condition of such release, periodic examinations of the defendant as to his competency. . . . If the court finds that the defendant has attained competency, he shall be returned to the custody of the Commissioner of Correction or released . . . and the court shall continue with the criminal proceedings" (Competency to Stand Trial, 2000).

Throughout the Kenneth Curtis case, the social worker from the Bridgeport Office of Court Evaluations served as an intricate part of the forensic team assigned to determine his competency. The social worker functioned as an equal member of the forensic team in gathering collateral information, evaluating Mr. Curtis's presentation, and preparing and reviewing the report that led to the legal opinion regarding Mr. Curtis's competency.

REFERENCES

Competency to Stand Trial (1995). *Connecticut General Statute* Volume 13, §54-56d, p. 830.

Competency to Stand Trial (1998). *Connecticut General Statute* Volume 13, §54-56d(m).

Competency to Stand Trial (2000). *Connecticut General Statute* Volume 13, §54-56d(m).

Courts Diagnostic Clinic (1980). Procedure and Techniques, Competency to Stand Trial. *Policy and Procedure Manual,* 46-54.

Hanrahan, W. (1999). Competent Curtis Pleads Guilty. *New Haven Register,* September 17, p. A1.

State of Connecticut v. Kenneth Curtis, Superior Court Judicial District of Fairfield at Bridgeport (1989, May 25). Competency Evaluation.

State of Connecticut v. Kenneth Curtis, Superior Court Judicial District of Fairfield at Bridgeport (1999). Competence to Stand Trial Evaluation, March 17, p. 27.

State of Connecticut v. Kenneth Curtis, Superior Court Judicial District of Fairfield at Bridgeport (1999, August 3). Decision RE: Competency to Stand Trial.

Stratford Police Arrest Warrant (1988). January 19.

Stratford Police Arrest Warrant (1997). November 3.

Tepfer, D. (1999). Curtis: 20 years. *Connecticut Post,* December 4, p. A1.

Chapter 3

Stalking: The Current Science

Shayna Gothard

DEFINITION

Stalking refers to a behavioral pattern of repeated and unwanted pursuits of another person. The behavior is statutorily defined as opposed to psychiatrically defined. Although stalking and stalkinglike behavior have been in existence for quite some time, it became criminalized only in 1990. California was the first state to pass antistalking legislation, utilizing the following legal definition of a stalker: "Any person who willfully, maliciously, and repeatedly follows or harasses another person and who makes a credible threat with the intent to place that person in reasonable fear for his or her safety or the safety of his or her immediate family" (Penal Code 646.9). By 1995, all states had passed some form of stalking legislation, and in 1996, federal laws prohibiting interstate stalking went into effect.

Although antistalking legislation exists nationwide, there are slight variations in the way in which stalking is defined (Tjaden and Thoennes, 1997). Some state statutes specify the minimum number of acts the alleged stalker must commit, whereas other statutes differ in terms of the threat and fear requirements. The wording of the California law captures the repetitious, unwanted behavior of the pursuer but has proved to be limiting in its threat component. That is, because most stalkers do not actually threaten their victims, prosecutors are frequently unable to charge the pursuer with stalking. Instead, perpetrators who engage in stalkinglike behavior but do not voice threats are frequently charged with related offenses such as violating a restraining order, making harassing phone calls, or, if there is violence, assault. Therefore, it has been recommended that the threat requirement be removed from all state statutes (Tjaden and Thoennes, 1997). Despite this statutory limitation, the overriding positive issue is the widespread consensus that stalking is and should be treated as criminal behavior.

PREVALENCE

The best estimate of the prevalence of stalking is based on the results of the National Violence Against Women Survey, a large study funded by the National Institute of Justice and the Center for Disease Control and Prevention. This study was conducted between November 1995 and May 1996 and included telephone surveys of 8,000 men and 8,000 women across the United States. The purpose of the study, in part, was to determine the lifetime victimization rates of stalking. Stalking was defined as "a course of conduct directed at a specific person that involves repeated visual or physical proximity, nonconsensual communication, or verbal, written, or implied threats, or a combination thereof, that would cause a reasonable person fear, with 'repeated' meaning on two or more occasions" (Tjaden and Thoennes, p. 2). The survey found that 8.1 percent of all women surveyed and 2.2 percent of all men surveyed had been the victim of stalking at least once in their lifetime (Tjaden and Thoennes, 1997). The authors determined that based on the U.S. Census Bureau population estimates, one out of every twelve women and one out of every forty-five men will be stalked at some point in their lifetime (Tjaden and Thoennes, 1997). These numbers unequivocally demonstrate that stalking occurs with much greater frequency than previously estimated.

DEMOGRAPHIC CHARACTERISTICS OF STALKERS

Empirically derived research on the demographic constitution of stalkers consistently demonstrates that they are predominantly males in their mid-thirties to early forties (Meloy and Gothard, 1995; Mullen and Pathe, 1994b; Schwartz-Watts and Morgan, 1998; Zona, Sharma, and Lane, 1993). They frequently have an educational attainment of high school or above and average to above-average intellectual functioning (Meloy and Gothard, 1995; Kienlen et al., 1997; Schwartz-Watts, Morgan, and Barnes, 1997). Stalkers are also frequently unemployed or underemployed (Meloy and Gothard, 1995; Mullen and Pathe, 1994a), which could account for the excessive time they spend pursuing their victims. Stalkers are unlikely to be married (Meloy and Gothard, 1995; Mullen and Pathe, 1994b; Schwartz-Watts, Morgan, and Barnes, 1997; Zona, Sharma, and Lane, 1993) and more likely to have a history of some prior legal involvement (Meloy and Gothard, 1995; Harmon, Rosner, and Owens, 1995; Mullen and Pathe, 1994b). One study (Schwartz-Watts, Morgan, and Barnes, 1997) found that stalkers were likely to have a military history and a history of organicity, although these findings have yet to be replicated. In sum, the prototype stalker is a single, educated, unemployed or underemployed male, between the ages of thirty-five and forty, with a history of involvement within the legal system.

PSYCHIATRIC CHARACTERISTICS OF STALKERS

There is considerable variability regarding the psychiatric makeup of stalkers. Many have no diagnosable mental disorder while others have elaborate, entrenched delusions fueling their actions. In Meloy and Gothard's (1995) study of twenty "obsessional followers" referred for psychological evaluations, the most common psychiatric diagnoses were substance abuse/dependence, mood disorders, adjustment disorders, and schizophrenia. Erotomanic delusional disorders occurred only in 10 percent of the population, a percentage mirrored by another study of stalkers (Zona, Sharma, and Lane, 1993). When there were AXIS II diagnoses, the most common types of personality disorders were borderline, narcissistic, or unspecified (Meloy and Gothard, 1995). From this author's clinical experience, female stalkers tend to more frequently carry a diagnosis of a borderline personality disorder. This diagnosis appears intuitively fitting for stalkers, given that borderline personality disorder is characterized by interpersonal instability. Meloy and Gothard (1995) also found that stalkers were less likely than other offenders referred for mental health evaluations to be diagnosed with an antisocial personality disorder (ASPD). Viewed from an attachment theory perspective, these authors speculated that stalkers were less likely to have an antisocial diagnosis since ASPD is a disease of chronic emotional detachment, whereas stalkers exhibit a pattern of overattachment (Meloy and Gothard, 1995).

Defensively, stalkers tend to employ the mechanisms of denial, projection, projective identification, and minimization to account for their behavior (Kienlen et al., 1997; Meloy and Gothard, 1995). In demonstration of the degree of projection exhibited by stalkers, many have been known to take out restraining orders against their victims and to talk about feeling "victimized" or "harassed." An amazing lack of insight into their behavior is also characteristic of stalkers. For example, some stalkers continue to call their victims from jail or to appeal to their victims to serve as character witnesses in court.

The motivation to stalk ranges from a desire for reconciliation and reunion to revenge and intimidation (Mullen et al., 1999). Desires to maintain control over the victim or to instill fear are also common motivating factors. Less commonly, stalkers are driven by a psychotic belief system (Tjaden and Thoennes, 1997).

VICTIM-OFFENDER RELATIONSHIP

The relationship between stalkers and their victims is most commonly grouped into three categories: (1) a current or former intimate relationship between stalker and victim, (2) an acquaintanceship between stalker and victim, and (3) no prior relationship (i.e., strangers) between stalker and victim.

Females, the more common stalking victim, are significantly more likely to be stalked by current or former intimates than by acquaintances or strangers (Tjaden and Thoennes, 1997). Almost 60 percent of the women surveyed reported being stalked by an intimate partner. Attesting to the link between stalking and domestic violence, the National Violence Against Women Survey also found that for 79 percent of the women stalked by former intimates, the stalking either started or continued after the woman left the relationship. In contrast, only one-third of the males surveyed were stalked by former intimates. Research also suggests that when the stalkers and victims have a history of intimacy, the stalkers tend to be emotionally driven to engage in their pursuit, rather than motivated by delusional ideation (Tjaden and Thoennes, 1997).

Stalking also occurs in the context of people who are acquainted. For example, there have been cases of stalkers pursuing their bank tellers, their physicians, and their neighbors. In these scenarios, the stalker is much more likely to be motivated by delusional ideation. For example, one woman whom this author evaluated had the delusional belief that her physician was in love with her. Her delusion was so fixed that she mailed out wedding invitations announcing their intent to marry. Research to date suggests that men are more likely to be victimized by acquaintances than are women (Tjaden and Thoennes, 1997).

The smallest group of stalkers and victims has no prior relationship; they are strangers. In the National Violence Against Women Survey, only 23 percent of females and 36 percent of males were stalked by strangers. The stranger scenario is common in situations involving movie stars, such as Madonna, David Letterman, and Steven Spielberg. Although the stalking of strangers occurs with considerably less frequency, the positive outcome of celebrity stalking is that the press it receives has increased national awareness of this crime.

STALKING TYPOLOGIES

Going beyond the victim-offender relationship, other researchers have proposed stalking typologies (Harmon, Rosner, and Owens, 1995; Mullen et al., 1999; Zona, Sharma, and Lane, 1993). Although most agree that there is an important distinction between the stalking of a prior intimate and the stalking of someone not previously involved with the perpetrator, there is less agreement regarding further subdivisions (Kamphuis and Emmelkamp, 2000). Zona and colleagues (1993) were the first to propose a stalking typology, which consisted of the following groups: simple obsessional, love obsessional, and erotomanic. The simple obsessional was defined as a stalker who had a prior relationship, romantic or otherwise, with the victim. The love obsessional group was defined as those lacking an existing relationship with their victim and who were typically psychotic, while the erotomanic group harbored psychotic delusions about their victim.

More recently, researchers have attempted to develop prototypes of stalkers based on the stalkers' behavior, motivation, and psychopathology (Mullen et al., 1999). Using a sample of 145 stalkers referred for psychiatric treatment, these authors proposed five prototypes of stalking:

1. Rejected
2. Incompetent
3. Intimacy seeking
4. Resentful
5. Predatory

The rejected stalkers (n = 41) were typically prior intimates of their victims, with their pursuits characterized by both revenge and a desire for reconciliation. These stalkers were also described as sad, frustrated, angry, jealous, and vindictive. The majority was diagnosed with personality disorders. Intimacy seekers (n = 27) were the second largest group of stalkers. This group included people with erotomanic delusions and others who were "morbidly infatuated" with their victims. These stalkers were predominantly motivated by a desire to establish a relationship with the victims and were frequently diagnosed with personality disorders. The incompetents (n = 22) were depicted as both socially incompetent and intellectually limited. They were noted to understand that their victim did not reciprocate their affection but were hopeful that their behavior would convince the victim otherwise. The resentful (n = 16) stalkers were predominantly driven to frighten and distress their victims. Some of the victims were known to them whereas others were chosen at random. The last group, the predators (n= 6), predominantly engaged in stalking behavior in preparation for a sexual attack. Many in this category were diagnosed with paraphilias and had prior convictions for sex offenses. Although this typology appears to have good discriminant validity, it has yet to be cross-validated on another sample.

There is not yet evidence that any one stalking typology is superior to the other. However, the current direction of research efforts supports the belief that there is a need to develop an agreed-upon stalking typology for both sentencing and treatment purposes.

PATTERNS OF PURSUIT

Unfortunately, stalkers tend to engage in multiple and various types of pursuits rather than single venues (Meloy and Gothard, 1995; Tjaden and Thoennes, 1997). The stalker who singularly writes letters or leaves phone messages is rare. Instead, stalkers are more likely to make both indirect and direct contacts that tend to increase in frequency and intensity over time. Some of the pursuit behaviors in which stalkers engage include appearing at a victim's home, appearing at a victim's work, following in a vehicle, telephoning, vandalizing property, sending letters, sending gifts, and threatening to harm the family pet (Tjaden and Thoennes, 1997). Stalkers have also been known to engage in indirect harassment such as ordering goods on the victim's behalf, initiating false legal actions, and relaying false and frequently disparaging information to third parties. For example, one stalker contacted his victim's boss and informed the boss that the victim was a drug abuser. Another stalker ordered expensive furniture and charged it to the victim's credit card, and yet another sued the victim civilly. Stalkers have also been known to go through their victims' mail, enter their home and move furniture about, steal personal items, bug their telephone, and even file false police reports (Hall, 1998).

Stalking by means of the Internet (i.e., cyberstalking) appears to be increasing with frequency, likely due to the popularity of communicating via electronic mail (e-mail) (Deirmenjian, 1999). Cyberstalking can take the form of individual e-mails directed at the victim or e-mails directed at specific groups. For example, there was a case in Southern California in which a University of California student sent threatening messages to fifty-nine Asian students. Cyberstalkers have also been known to provide personal and frequently false information about their victims online and to place "for a good time, call" advertisements on the Internet with the victim's information used.

Attesting to their above-average intelligence (Meloy and Gothard, 1995), stalkers can be extremely resourceful in terms of eliciting confidential information. One stalker known to this author went to the department of motor vehicles, posed as a police officer, and was able to obtain the unlisted phone number of his victim. Others have been known to circumvent phone blocks and to engage in harassing behaviors that are just short of being illegal.

The duration of stalking can vary from months to years with an average pursuit length of 1.8 years (Tjaden and Thoennes, 1997). When the perpetrator is an intimate or former intimate, the pursuit lasts significantly longer than when the perpetrator is a nonintimate. The average pursuit by a former intimate is 2.2 years versus 1.1 years by a nonintimate (Tjaden and Thoennes, 1997). Unfortunately, stalking does not necessarily end with a conviction. The offender may continue to send letters from jail or even phone the victim collect while incarcerated.

VIOLENCE: THREATS AND INCIDENCE

Although in many states a threat of harm is necessary for someone to be charged with stalking, research indicates that less than one-half of the stalkers actually threaten their victims (Tjaden and Thoennes, 1997). Fortunately, most stalkers do not follow through with their threats, and actual acts of violence are usually preceded by threats. However, an absence of threats should not give a victim a false sense of safety.

There is a greater likelihood of threats and violence if the stalker and victim were previously involved (Kienlen et al., 1997; Meloy and Gothard, 1995; Schwartz-Watts and Morgan, 1998; Tjaden and Thoennes, 1997). In the National Violence Against Women Survey, 81 percent of the women who were stalked by former husbands or former partners were physically assaulted. Stalking husbands were estimated to be four times more likely than husbands or partners in the general population to assault their partners. Threats are also more likely to be made by stalkers who are not psychotic (Kienlen et al., 1997). Thus, although we are likely to be more fearful of psychotic stalkers because their behavior can be more bizarre, in actuality they are less violent.

Fortunately, most cases of violence do not result in physical injury and do not involve weapons. When property violence occurs, it is most frequently directed at cars (Meloy et al., 2000). The actual incidence of homicide is estimated to occur in less than 2 percent of the cases (Meloy, 1996), though we do not know how many homicide victims may have been stalked before they were killed. When violence does occur, it is most likely to be assault and battery without a weapon, such as the victim being grabbed, punched, struck, or fondled. If a weapon is utilized, it is most commonly a knife, gun, or car (Meloy et al., 2000).

VICTIM CHARACTERISTICS

Anyone can be a victim of stalking. However, women have a substantially greater risk of being stalked than do men. In the National Violence Against Women Survey, four out of five stalking victims were female. The age bracket most afflicted by stalking appears to be young adults, between the ages of eighteen and thirty-nine. The average age of the victims at the onset of the stalking was twenty-eight and the overwhelming majority was stalked by one person (Tjaden and Thoennes, 1997). The survey also found that only 28 percent of the female victims and 10 percent of the male victims took out restraining orders against their stalker, though most of the stalkers violated the orders. Of further concern was the finding that only 52 percent of the female victims and 45 percent of the male victims reported their stalking to the police (Tjaden and Thoennes, 1997).

Psychologically, stalking has a profound effect on the victims (Hall, 1998; Pathe and Mullen, 1997). There is an incredible sense of intrusion, helplessness, and boundary violation when one is stalked. Many report psychological symptoms such as anxiety, sleep disturbances, overwhelming powerlessness, and flashbacks. Sometimes, their symptomatology is so severe as to warrant a diagnosis of post-traumatic stress disorder (Pathe and Mullen, 1997). Stalking victims also report tremendous upheaval in their lives secondary to their victimization. Many indicate that they modify their activities as a means of avoiding places the stalker might frequent, reduce their social outings, change or cease employment, obtain additional security measures and/or move. Other victims report feeling less trusting, feeling easily frightened, leading more isolated lives, and behaving more aggressively (Hall, 1998). Unfortunately, the psychological impact of being stalked appears to extend beyond the cessation of the actual victimization.

RISK MANAGEMENT STRATEGIES

Although stalking is never the fault of the victim, it is important for the victim to assume the responsibility of his or her safety (Meloy, 1997). Victims should maintain a log of all current and past actions of the stalker. This includes saving voice and electronic messages, packages, letters, and other items sent by the perpetrator. It is also important to document each incident of stalking, such as when the stalker is seen driving by one's home or work.

Alerting family, friends, and colleagues of the stalker and enlisting their support to document stalking incidents is also recommended. The issue of obtaining a restraining order is more complicated. On the one hand, it can give the victims a sense of well-being to take out a restraining order and potentially help with the stalkers' arrest. However, it can also further escalate violence in a small percentage of perpetrators (Meloy, 1997). Nevertheless, it is generally recommended that victims obtain a restraining order (Meloy, 1997). Other risk management strategies include changing door locks and obtaining a second phone line for family and friends. Changing one's daily schedule and routine is also recommended. Although the victim may be tempted to have contact with the stalker, believing it will satiate the stalker's desire for contact, this only serves to reinforce the stalker's behavior (Meloy, 1997). Therefore, it is recommended that the victim cease all contact with the stalker. Finally, it is important to treat all threats of violence as legitimate and alert the police of any threatening or illegal behavior, including any violations of a restraining order.

REFERENCES

Deirmenjian, J.M. (1999). Stalking in cyberspace. *Journal of the American Academy of Psychiatry and the Law,* 27(3), 407-413.

Hall, D.M. (1998). The victims of stalking. In Meloy, J.R. (Ed.), *Psychology of Stalking* (pp. 113-136). San Diego, CA: Academic Press.

Harmon, R.B., Rosner, R., and Owens, H. (1995). Obsessional harassment and erotomania in a criminal court population. *Journal of Forensic Sciences,* 40(3), 188-196.

Kamphuis, J.H. and Emmelkamp, P.M.G. (2000). Stalking—A contemporary challenge for forensic and clinical psychiatry. *British Journal of Psychiatry,* 176, 206-209.

Kienlen, K.K., Birmingham, D.L., Solberg, K.B., Oregan, J.T., and Meloy, J.R. (1997). A comparative study of psychotic and nonpsychotic stalking. *Journal of the American Academy of Psychiatry and the Law,* 25(3), 317-334.

Meloy, J.R. (1996). Stalking (obsessional following): A review of some preliminary studies. *Aggression and Violent Behavior,* 1(2), 147-162.

Meloy, J.R. (1997). The clinical risk management of stalking: "Someone is watching over me . . .". *American Journal of Psychotherapy,* 51(2), 175-184.

Meloy, J.R. and Gothard, S. (1995). Demographic and clinical comparison of obsessional followers and offenders with mental disorders. *American Journal of Psychiatry,* 152(2), 258-263.

Meloy, J.R., Rivers, L., Siegel, L., Gothard, S., Naimark, D., and Nicolini, J.R. (2000). A replication study of obsessional followers and offenders with mental disorders. *Journal of Forensic Sciences,* 45(1), 147-152.

Mullen, P.E. and Pathe, M. (1994a). The pathological extensions of love. *British Journal of Psychiatry,* 165, 614-623.

Mullen, P.E. and Pathe, M. (1994b). Stalking and the pathologies of love. *Australian and New Zealand Journal of Psychiatry,* 28(3), 469-477.

Mullen, P.E., Pathe, M., Purcell, R., and Stuart, G.W. (1999). Study of stalkers. *American Journal of Psychiatry,* 156(8), 1244-1249.

Pathe, M. and Mullen, P.E. (1997). The impact of stalkers on their victims. *British Journal of Psychiatry,* 170, 12-17.

Schwartz-Watts, D. and Morgan, D.W. (1998). Violent versus nonviolent stalkers. *Journal of the American Academy of Psychiatry and the Law,* 26(2), 241-245.

Schwartz-Watts, D., Morgan, D.W., and Barnes, C.J. (1997). Stalkers: The South Carolina experience. *Journal of the American Academy of Psychiatry and the Law,* 25(4), 541-545.

Tjaden, P. and Thoennes, N. (1997). *Stalking in America: Findings from the National Violence Against Women Survey.* Denver, CO: Center for Policy Research.

Zona, M.A., Sharma, K.K., and Lane, J. (1993). A comparative study of erotomanic and obsessional subjects in a forensic sample. *Journal of Forensic Sciences,* 38(4), 894-903.

Chapter 4

Links Among Animal Abuse, Child Abuse, and Domestic Violence

Barbara W. Boat

ANIMAL ABUSE

We start with the topic of animal abuse because, historically, this is where an organized approach to dealing with child abuse began. In New York City, in 1874, an extremely abused child named Mary Ellen was rescued, in part, by appealing to the Society for the Prevention of Cruelty to Animals (SPCA). The SPCA advocated for Mary Ellen in the court system, as no similar society was available to protect children. This newsworthy event led to establishing the first Society for the Prevention of Cruelty to Children (SPCC).

Significant data document associations between animal abuse and various forms of interpersonal violence (see Lockwood and Ascione, 1998). Many perpetrators of recent school shootings in the United States abused animals. Individuals with a history of being prosecuted for animal abuse are three to five times more likely to have been arrested for violent offenses against humans as well as property crimes and drug-related offenses (Arluke et al., 1999). In Lucas County, Ohio, a summary of the rap sheets of fourteen men convicted of fighting pit bulls revealed numerous other violations, including 206 vehicle traffic offenses, five aggravated trafficking in drugs, thirteen outstanding warrants, and five carrying concealed weapons.

"Violence to people and animals" is a leading symptom of conduct disorder in the *Diagnostic and Statistical Manual of Mental Disorders* of the American Psychiatric Association (DSM-IV). Cruelty to animals is the earliest symptom of conduct disorder in children, appearing around six years of age. Thus, it can be very important to ask about children's interactions with animals and take seriously any cruel behaviors reported, especially behaviors that appear to be a deliberate infliction of pain and suffering on the animal that provides the child with gratification.

At the same time, our concern about animal cruelty, especially when manifested by children, needs to be counterbalanced with an understanding of child development and the possible motivations for exhibiting aggressive or cruel behaviors toward animals. The motivations can be complex and multidetermined. For example, young children may be curious and experimental, unaware that poking, choking, stepping on, kicking, or restraining an animal is harmful. Many times no adult is monitoring these behaviors and providing the necessary teaching and restraint. Peer reinforcement for "showing off" or "daring" can lead to acts of cruelty that a child would not perform if alone. Tying a cat to a railroad track or throwing it over a cliff to win peer approval does not necessarily mean the child will harm his or her own pets. Children also will imitate aggressive behaviors toward animals if this is what has been modeled.

Children can harm or kill another's pet to retaliate against a sibling or address a grievance. We also must keep in mind that species prejudice may mitigate the act in the mind of the child. For example, "It was only a cat" or "It was just a stray."

Sometimes children's abusive behaviors toward pets may be a form of posttraumatic reenactment. Recent research indicates that children who have been maltreated are more likely to be reported as cruel to animals than nonmaltreated children. The highest risk children were those who were both physically and sexually abused (34 percent were cruel to animals) and physically abused (25.5 percent). The rate of reported animal cruelty in nonabused children was 4.7 percent (Ascione, 2001). We can speculate that trauma-based symptoms interfere with the development of empathy and impulsivity control.

CHILD ABUSE

Animal welfare programs throughout the United States recognized the links between animal and child welfare long before professionals working with children did so. However, relatively little research documents this link. The most cited work is that of DeViney, Dickert, and Lockwood (1983). They found that 83 percent of homes with abused or neglected children also had abused and neglected pets. Knowledge of this relationship has led to several screening and early intervention or prevention approaches.

Cross-Training of Child Protection Workers and Animal Control Officers

In California, animal protection workers are mandated reporters of child abuse and receive special training in recognizing and reporting child abuse and neglect. Animal control officers frequently get calls concerning animal neglect. Animals and humans often share a neglectful environment, and because the officers can go to a premise unannounced, they have the unique opportunity to see the deplorable conditions and initiate interventions that can benefit the entire family. Animal control officers are also carefully trained investigators whose reports of child abuse or neglect are usually substantiated. Unfortunately, child protection workers are less likely to use animal neglect or cruelty to advocate for a client's welfare. Hopefully, they will eventually find it is useful to check out the pets when they check out the kids.

Screening Children for Animal-Related Experiences

Asking children routinely about pets can be a window on the child's home life and illuminate risks that might otherwise go undetected. Samples of types of questions that can be asked include:

- Do you have pets or other animals at your house?
- What kind? What are their names?
- Who takes care of ___________?
- Does anyone hurt ____________? (or) Does _______ ever get hurt?
- How? By whom?
- How is ________ disciplined (trained, taught to be good, etc.)?
- Have you ever lost a pet or animal that you really cared about? What happened?
- Do you ever worry about something bad happening to your pet or another animal?

A ten-question form of the Boat Inventory on Animal-Related Experiences that can be given to children, adolescents, or adults is included at the end of this chapter. The expanded interview protocol is reprinted in my chapter in Ascione and Arkow (1999).

Experiences with Animals May Have Major Treatment and Intervention Implications

The loss of a pet can be a lifelong source of pain. One psychiatrist reported treating a Vietnam vet who told him, “Doctor, I went through hell in Vietnam, but the thing that bothers me the most is, when I was a kid, my dad killed my dog.” Likewise, children who witness domestic violence may be very distraught if a pet is left behind when they are forced to seek shelter, usually with their mothers. In one powerful, recorded 911 emergency phone call, a six-year-old girl’s mother was shot and killed while the child was making the phone call. Early in the call, the girl sobbed, “My cat’s scared, too!” The question we are left with is whether anyone heard her concern for her cat and considered how important it could be therapeutically to let the child know that someone had provided a safe place for the cat and, if possible, arrange for the child to see her cat.

Attachment to a pet may be exploited to coerce or control another’s behavior. For some children and adults, just the threat of loss is enough to force compliance. Jennifer was six years old when her mother remarried and, almost immediately, her stepfather began to molest her sexually. He was having intercourse with her by the time she was eight. Jennifer lived in an isolated, rural, mountain region; her horses were her closest companions. When Jennifer began to protest the sexual assaults, her stepfather threatened to have her horses killed. She remained compliant to save her horses, then brought charges against him when she went away to college.

Sexually reactive children who have been abused may use pets as sources of sexual stimulation. It can be important to alert caregivers to this possibility to avoid later tragedies. In one case, a seven-year-old girl had recently disclosed her molestation by a neighbor, and her mother was still understandably distraught. When the mother heard her daughter moaning behind the closed bedroom door and entered the room, she discovered that the family cat was between her daughter's legs, licking her genitals. The enraged mother slammed the cat into the wall, killing it. Had the mother been forewarned, this devastating act might have been avoided.

Taking into account a child's experiences with pets can contribute to therapeutic interventions. A thirteen-year-old girl was severely beaten by her father. She had endured his rages since she was eight, but this time he nearly killed her. As we explored her relationships with pets, she began to cry. She recalled a time when her cat had been badly hurt by her father when he was angry and she was terribly worried about its safety. She also worried about the welfare of the two dogs, one a full-blooded wolf that her father kept on short chains in the yard. As part of her treatment, her social worker agreed to report the father to the local humane society. The father was cited for animal neglect. Later, the father reported that his daughter's cat had to be euthanized when the dogs attacked it. Most important, however, he agreed to find new homes for the dogs. Recently, the girl, who now lives with relatives, got a new kitten of her choosing that she brought to our session for a visit. Addressing the safety and well-being of her pets has enabled her to exert some control, and reinforce her feelings of empathy and caring during a time when she has been highly stressed.

DOMESTIC VIOLENCE

Pets live in almost 80 percent of the homes that have school-age children. Pets share the social interactions that occur in families. Thus, it comes as no surprise that pets, like children, are likely to be at risk in violent homes. In homes where people are abused, animals are abused, and vice versa.

In domestic violence cases, in which most victims are women, a batterer can use pets to establish power and control. It signals to the woman that there is no safe place for her or her pet; it threatens, or actually destroys, a source of comfort and support; it provides the batterer with the opportunity to gain compliance; it is a mechanism to instill terror as the batterer may torture the pet or another animal in front of the adult victim and children; abusive behaviors toward pets can prevent the victim from seeking shelter sooner because of fear of what will happen to the pets if left behind.

Animal abuse on the part of the batterer is considered an indicator of potential lethality, along with suicidal and homicidal threats and having a weapon. The most violent batterers in one study were those who tended to behave sadistically toward pets (Jacobson and Gottman, 1998).

When domestic violence is suspected, victims who have, or have had, pets need to be questioned routinely about the following:

- Has your partner ever threatened to harm your pet?
- Has your partner ever hurt or killed your pet?
- Has your partner ever hurt or tortured another animal to instill fear in you or your children?
- Have your children ever witnessed harm to your pet?
- Have your children ever harmed or killed a pet or deliberately hurt other animals?
- Did concerns about your pet's welfare keep you from seeking shelter or help sooner?

In a study by Ascione (1998), the pet-related experiences of 101 women who were battered and entered crisis shelters were compared with pet-related experiences of sixty women who had not experienced domestic violence. Seventy-two percent of the battered women reported that their partners had threatened to harm or actually harmed their pets. In contrast, 14.5 percent of nonbattered women reported such behaviors. Actual hurting or killing of pets by partners was reported by 54 percent of the battered women and 3.5 percent of nonbattered women. Over half of the children of the battered mothers reported that they tried to protect their pets when violence erupted. Nearly one in four of the battered women said that concern for their pets' welfare prevented them from seeking shelter sooner. As one poster from the Washington Humane Society reads: "The man who comes home and kicks the dog may be just warming up."

The elderly are also vulnerable to crimes of domestic violence and may have money or other items extorted through threats to harm their pets.

A CALL TO CONNECT

During the past decade, we have witnessed an upsurge of cooperative efforts between professionals who deal with people and professionals who deal with animals. Routine screening of animal-related experiences enables professionals to obtain additional, often vital, information. This information can alert battered women's shelters to seek pet-sheltering services for their clients, especially if women are delaying leaving their partners because of concerns about their pets' welfare. Knowledge of animal-related experiences can be useful in the courtroom or in advocacy work to help assess risk in both children and adults. Cross-training animal control professionals and children's protection workers can result in earlier detection and interventions for both humans and animals. Mandated reporting of animal abuse and child abuse by veterinarians and animal control officers can assist this effort.

By being aware of the links, we can collect data to inform creative interventions and programs to reduce violence in the lives of humans and animals.

APPENDIX: BOAT INVENTORY ON ANIMAL-RELATED EXPERIENCES

Ten Screening Questions for Children, Adolescents, and Adults

1. Have you or your family ever had a pet(s)? _ _ _ _ _ _ _ _ _ _ Y N

	How many?
a. Dog(s)	________
b. Cat(s)	________
c. Bird(s)	________
d. Fish	________
e. Horse(s)	________
f. Turtles, snakes, lizards, insects, etc.	________
g. Rabbits, hamsters, mice, guinea pigs, gerbils	________
h. Wild animals (describe)______________	________
i. Other (describe)____________________	________

2. Do you have a pet or pets now? _ _ _ _ _ _ _ _ _ _ _ _ _ _ _ Y N

	How many?
a. Dog(s)	________
b. Cat(s)	________
c. Bird(s)	________
d. Fish	________
e. Horse(s)	________
f. Turtles, snakes, lizards, insects, etc.	________
g. Rabbits, hamsters, mice, guinea pigs, gerbils	________
h. Wild animals (describe)______________	________
i. Other (describe)____________________	________

3. Did you ever have a favorite or special pet? _ _ _ _ _ _ _ _ Y N

What kind?____

Why was the pet special?______________________________________

4. Has a pet ever been a source of comfort or support to you—even if you did not own the pet? (e.g., When you were sad or scared?) _ _ Y N

How old were you?____

a. Under age 6
b. 6-12 years
c. Teenager
d. Adult

Describe the pet and what happened. ______________________________

____

____

5. Has your pet ever been hurt? _ _ _ _ _ _ _ _ _ _ _ _ _ _ _ Y N

What happened? (describe)_____________________________________

____

____

a. Accidental? (hit by car, attacked by another animal, fell, ate something, etc.)
b. Deliberate? (kicked, punched, thrown, not fed, etc.)

6. Have you ever felt afraid for your pet or worried about bad things happening to your pet? (describe) _ _ _ _ _ _ _ _ _ _ _ _ _ _ Y N

____

____

Are you worried now? _ _ _ _ _ _ _ _ _ _ _ _ _ _ _ _ _ _ Y N

7. Have you ever lost a pet you really cared about? (e.g., Was given away, ran away, died, or was somehow killed?) _ _ _ _ _ _ Y N

What kind of pet?____

If your pet died, was the death:
a. Natural (old age, illness, euthanized)
b. Accidental (hit by car)
c. Deliberate (strangled, drowned)
d. Cruel or violent (e.g., pet was tortured)

What happened?

____
____
____

Was the death or loss used to punish you or make you do something?
_ Y N

How difficult was the loss for you?
a. Not difficult
b. Somewhat difficult
c. Very difficult

How much does it bother you now?
a. Not at all
b. Somewhat
c. A lot

How did people react/what did they tell you after you lost your pet?
a. Supportive
b. Said it was your fault
c. Punished you
d. Other______________

How old were you?
a. Under age 6
b. 6-12 years
c. Teenager
d. Adult

8. Have you ever *seen* someone hurt an animal or pet? _ _ _ _ _ Y N

How many?

a. Dog(s) ___________
b. Cat(s) ___________
c. Bird(s) ___________
d. Fish ___________
e. Horse(s) ___________
f. Turtles, snakes, lizards, insects, etc. ___________
g. Rabbits, hamsters, mice, guinea pigs, gerbils ___________
h. Wild animals (describe)______________ ___________
i. Other (describe)____________________ ___________

What did they do?

a. Drowned
b. Hit, beat, kicked
c. Stoned
d. Shot (BB gun, bow and arrow)
e. Strangled
f. Stabbed
g. Burned
h. Starved or neglected
i. Trapped
j. Had sex with it
k. Other (describe)____________________________________

Was it
a. accidental?
b. deliberate?
c. coerced?

How old were you? *(circle all that apply)*

a. Under age 6
b. 6-12 years
c. Teenager
d. Adult

Were they hunting the animal for food or sport?_ _ _ _ _ _ Y N

Did anyone know they did this? _ _ _ _ _ _ _ _ _ _ _ _ _ _ _ _ _ Y N

What happened afterward?________________________________

____

9. Have *you* ever hurt an animal or pet _ _ _ _ _ _ _ _ _ _ _ _ _ _ Y N

	How many?
a. Dog(s)	________
b. Cat(s)	________
c. Bird(s)	________
d. Fish	________
e. Horse(s)	________
f. Turtles, snakes, lizards, insects, etc.	________
g. Rabbits, hamsters, mice, guinea pigs, gerbils	________
h. Wild animals (describe)______________	________
i. Other (describe)__________________	________

What did you do?

a. Drowned
b. Hit, beat, kicked
c. Stoned
d. Shot (BB gun, bow and arrow)
e. Strangled
f. Stabbed
g. Burned
h. Starved or neglected
i. Trapped
j. Had sex with it
k. Other (describe)________________________________

Was it

a. accidental?
b. deliberate?
c. coerced?

How old were you? *(circle all that apply)*

a. Under age 6
b. 6-12 years

c. Teenager
d. Adult

Were you hunting the animal for food or sport? _ _ _ _ _ _ _ _ Y N

Were you alone when you did this?_ _ _ _ _ _ _ _ _ _ _ _ _ _ _ _ Y N

Did anyone know you did this? _ _ _ _ _ _ _ _ _ _ _ _ _ _ _ _ _ Y N

What happened afterward?______________________________

____

10. Have you ever been frightened—really scared or hurt by an animal or pet? _ Y N

What happened?___________________________________

____

Are you still afraid of this kind of animal or other animals? _ _ Y N

____

Describe____

____

Demographics

Date: _______ Current grade or highest grade completed______
Date of birth: _______ Gender: Male____ Female ____
Age: _____ _____
(years) (months)

Ethnic Group:

Caucasian	_____	Asian	_____
African-American	_____	Hispanic	_____
Native-American	_____	Appalachian	_____
		Other____________	

Maternal level of education (highest grade completed)_______

The Childhood Trust CN-PAW, Department of Psychiatry ML 0539, University of Cincinnati, Cincinnati, OH 45267, (513) 558-9007, (513) 558-4107 (fax), <barbara.boat@uc.edu>.

REFERENCES

American Psychiatric Association (1994). *Diagnostic and Statistical Manual of Mental Disorders* (Fourth edition). Washington, DC: American Psychiatric Association.

Arluke, A., Levin, J., Luke, C., and Ascione, F. (1999). The relationship of animal abuse to violence and other forms of antisocial behavior. *Journal of Interpersonal Violence,* 14(9), 963-975.

Ascione, F.R. (1998). Battered women's reports of their partners' and their children's cruelty to animals. *Journal of Emotional Abuse,* 1(1), 119-133.

Ascione, F.R. (2001). Animal abuse and youth violence. *Juvenile Justice Bulletin,* OJJDP, NCS 188677, Washington, DC.

Ascione, F.R. and Akow, P. (Eds.) (1999). *Child abuse, domestic violence, and animal abuse: Linking the circles of compassion for prevention and intervention.* West Lafayette, IN: Purdue University Press.

DeViney, E., Dickert, J., and Lockwood, R. (1983). The care of pets within child abusing families. *International Journal for the Study of Animal Problems,* 4, 321-329.

Jacobson, N.S. and Gottman, J.M. (1998). *When men batter women.* New York: Simon and Schuster.

Lockwood, R. and Ascione, F. (Eds.) (1998). *Cruelty to animals and interpersonal violence: Readings in research and application.* West Lafayette, IN: Purdue University Press.

Chapter 5

Empowering Drug Courts Through Evaluation: Serving As Change Agents to Help Others Help Themselves

Julie Schroeder
Angela Trainham

A powerful movement toward judicial involvement in substance abuse treatment began in Miami, Florida, in 1989 to address the impact of crack cocaine and other drugs on the criminal justice system. Drug courts are rapidly emerging throughout the country. There are 455 drug courts operating in the United States, with another 287 programs in the planning stage of development. To date, approximately 140,000 people are currently participating or have graduated from drug court programs since their inception in the early 1990s. Retention rates for drug court programs is reported to be 70 percent (*Office of Justice Programs,* 2000).

The two primary goals of a drug court are to decrease the rates of relapse and recidivism. Relapse is defined as continued substance use after entering treatment. Recidivism is the commission of additional offenses and being returned to the criminal justice system for adjudication and sentencing if found guilty.

Though most of these programs are in their infancy, funding agents want proof of results now. Thus, programs are being developed and implemented with their sights on the results—decreased recidivism. However, many programs have been implemented quickly—perhaps too quickly. With an eye on the results, program developers have overlooked the quality of the implementation process. Appropriately implemented programs are vital to successful outcomes, yet there is no literature addressing the drug court implementation process or the problems associated with it.

Louisiana's first drug court was implemented in St. Mary Parish in June 1997. Currently, the state has thirty-one operating drug courts (twenty adult and eleven juvenile), and six jurisdictions are planning to implement drug courts in the year 2000. The Louisiana State University School of Social Work, Office of Social Service Research and Development (OSSRD) has a long history with the state's drug courts involving program planning, grant writing, and evaluation. For the 1999-2000 fiscal year, the Louisiana Department of Health and Hospitals Office for Addictive Disorders (OAD) contracted with OSSRD to provide process evaluation services to the drug courts statewide. OSSRD planned to conduct a combination of empowerment and traditional process evaluations.

DEVELOPMENT AND OPERATION OF THE DRUG COURT TEAM

A drug court program requires the integration of two different entities—the judicial system and the substance abuse treatment system. Integration is no small task. Drug court teams typically include judges, district attorneys, public defenders, substance abuse treatment professionals, and administrative coordinators. The marriage of the two systems requires a great deal of coordination, collaboration, and communication among team members. The way in which these two distinct groups work together will determine the success of a program. According to Bruce Tuckman and Mary Jensen (1977), team development is not a random process but evolves in specific stages.

Stages of Team Group Development

At the beginning of the OSSRD statewide drug court evaluation, the courts were at different stages of development ranging from a mature "mentor" court in St. Mary Parish to courts accepting their first referrals. The evaluation team was to perform both evaluation and monitoring functions for the courts as suggested by the Center for Substance Abuse Treatment (CSAT). Monitoring by periodic observation was to ensure that individual courts met the Louisiana drug court treatment standards and adhered to the U.S. Department of Justice's Drug Courts Program Office's (DCPO) ten key components of drug courts. Ongoing technical assistance, identifying training needs, and assistance in organizing training were built into the monitoring process.

The DCPO requires courts funded by them to have all members of the teams attend on-site training before they receive funds. The emphasis on the drug court team is consistent in all drug court literature. The OSSRD evaluation team members suggested that drug court teams experience the same developmental stages of other groups and, therefore, attempted to facilitate successful transitions between stages when problems were identified.

Stage One: Forming

This is a period of orientation and getting acquainted. Interpersonal behaviors are tested, and basic rules are developed. In the forming stage of drug courts, team members are identified; they have to "buy in" to the drug court process. Considerable commitment is required of judges, district attorneys, public defenders, probation officers, and treatment providers. As team members are recruited, attend out-of-state training, and plan sessions together, they bond about the common goals of drug court. They are excited about being part of a "movement" that is helping addicts stay out of the criminal justice system.

During this phase, the OSSRD evaluators participated in the planning committees in the courts. The evaluators provided topical research information, assisted in the evaluation design, and facilitated communication among professionals from different perspectives. The courts that do not successfully negotiate this stage do not form a bond strong enough to carry them through later stages. Problems during this time include not being able to bring in a key player or being unable to resolve power struggles among players.

Stage Two: Storming

At this point, individual personalities begin to emerge, and conflict and disagreement begin to occur. As the drug court begins to implement the plans developed in the forming stage, natural problems become evident. Issues that may have been easy to compromise in theory are harder in practice. Blaming may occur when clients do not succeed as planned.

Team members have to adjust professional perspectives and procedures. For example, prosecutors and defense attorneys on drug court teams are to have "nonadversarial" roles in the drug court process. Probation officers and clinicians have to compromise points of view about how and when to sanction a client for relapsing. Relapse is a natural part of recovery for the clinician, but a probation violation for the probation officer. As the team leader, the judge has the final authority to make decisions, and this requires a balanced approach between valuing each team member's contribution and making the ultimate decision.

Conflicts naturally occur as teams work out these issues. The more open and honest the disputes are, the easier it is to resolve them. The OSSRD evaluators provided ongoing conflict resolution as issues developed and facilitated team-building workshops as needed. Evaluators attempted to keep the team focused on problem solving instead of blaming, and stressed the necessity of conflict in the group process, encouraging the team to work through issues.

If successfully resolved, this stage makes the team stronger, and outcomes for clients should reflect this. Some courts in Louisiana have worked through this stage. Some continue to struggle to overcome conflict. One court completely disbanded and reformed with new key players when they could not successfully transverse this stage. The OSSRD evaluation team used the empowerment model of evaluation to assist the newly formed court to prepare for and resolve their implementation issues.

Stage Three: Norming

At this point of group development, conflict dissipates and is replaced with team harmony. Unity begins to evolve. Some courts evaluated by OSSRD were in the norming phase. Conflicts had been resolved, and the teams were working well together. OSSRD validated the process in place and assisted with technical needs identified by the courts.

Stage Four: Performing

At this point, the focus is directed toward mission development and attainment of goals. Commitment to team goals becomes evident, and individual roles are accepted. The courts evaluated by the OSSRD that were in the performing stage were outcome focused. These courts were interested in evaluating their programs to refine the drug court process to positively effect client outcomes.

If a group does not progress through these stages, team development suffers. Hellriegal, Slocum, and Woodman (1995) have identified specific group behaviors and dynamics that can directly affect outcomes. It is imperative that the evaluator understands the behaviors and dynamics to guide the emerging group in a positive direction.

THE NEXT STEP: EVALUATION

The process of integrating these two independent systems into a viable drug court program requires the efforts of all program participants. The empowerment model of evaluation is especially suited to drug courts at this stage of development to "help people help themselves and improve their programs using a form of self-evaluation and reflection" (Fetterman, Kaftarian, and Wandersman, 1996, p. 5).

Empowerment evaluation is defined as the use of "evaluation concepts, techniques, and findings to foster improvement and self-determination. . . . It is designed to help people help themselves and improve their programs using a form of self-evaluation and reflection" (Fetterman, Kaftarian, and Wandersman, 1996, p. 5). This model uses both qualitative and quantitative measures that can be applied to individuals, organizations, communities, societies, or cultures, with a focus on programs. This approach has been used in a wide variety of arenas including health, mental health, criminal justice, and education. It is not intended to replace other forms of evaluation.

Origins and Theoretical Framework

The foundation for this evaluation model is based on work in several areas. Empowerment evaluation can trace its evolutionary roots to community psychology, action anthropology, and collaborative and participatory evaluation. Examples include Bandura's (1982) work on self-efficacy and self-determination, Tax's (1996) focus on anthropologists' facilitation of goals and objectives of self-forming groups, and Rappaport's (1987) work emphasizing citizen participation and community development. Later work on collaborative and participatory evaluation, educational reform, and empowerment at the community level provided additional support for this model (Oja and Smulyan, 1989; Papineau and Kiely, 1994; Reason, 1988; Whitmore, 1990; Whyte, 1990).

Zimmerman's Empowerment Theory

This evaluation approach is based on Marc Zimmerman's "Empowerment Theory" (1987). He suggests that the empowerment process involves a person's attempt to gain control, obtain needed resources, and critically understand his or her social environment. "This experience is empowering if it helps people develop skills so they can become independent problem solvers and decision makers" (Zimmerman, p. 725). Often, this must be a collaborative effort.

In empowerment evaluation, a program's team members facilitate their own evaluation with evaluators acting as coaches. Evaluators become collaborators rather than serving as experts. The professional works with the team rather than advocating for them. Thus, the process becomes a collaborative, democratic group effort.

By instituting this type of self-evaluation, an organization's dynamic nature can be taken into consideration, and plans for program improvement take on a cyclical nature. Team members learn to continually assess their progress toward identified goals, and alter their course when necessary. In addition, identified goals and objectives are geared toward the "appropriate developmental level of implementation" (Fetterman, Kaftarian, and Wandersman, 1996, p. 6). This is especially important when considering drug courts. When a developmental continuum is taken into consideration, the evolution of a program is recognized, and outcomes are considered based on where the program is on the continuum. This allows for an appropriate level of expectation for new programs that have not yet been fully implemented, for young programs that show small gains, and for mature programs which show small gains or declines.

The Developmental Stages of Empowerment Evaluation

According to Fetterman, Kaftarian, and Wandersman's (1996) model, there are five specific facets—or stages—of empowerment evaluation. These include training, facilitation, advocacy, illumination, and liberation. Each stage is an integral part of the process.

Training

During the training phase of the process, evaluators teach program team members how to conduct their own evaluation. This helps to demystify the evaluation process and enables organizations to internalize evaluation principles and practices. Traditional evaluations tend to foster dependency. When a traditional evaluation ends, team members are left without the knowledge or the expertise to carry on. Empowerment evaluation is specifically designed to be ongoing and internalized in the program.

The primary focus of the training phase is to help team members establish an evaluation design by developing a preliminary assessment of program components, and a general overview of the program, highlighting strengths and weaknesses. This is accomplished largely through self-reflection. Once this has been done, team members are encouraged to establish goals and develop strategies to achieve them. The group then develops performance indicators and determines the best way in which to monitor progress toward those goals.

The training for drug courts funded by DCPO is mandated. Although there are some common evaluation components for drug courts, the OSSRD team employed an empowerment model in Louisiana. The OSSRD evaluators encouraged drug court teams to individualize the lessons learned in the training workshops and material to best fit their communities. The evaluators sought to have the team members internalize the need for evaluation and conceptualize how the programs could utilize evaluation results.

Facilitation

Evaluators must provide direction and information to keep the effort on course. Evaluators serve as coaches or facilitators, attending sessions to monitor the process, and provide general guidance. The program's team members are in charge of developing their own evaluation with the evaluator's assistance.

In the original scope of work, the OSSRD evaluation team was to facilitate the implementation of drug court programs by providing ongoing technical assistance and supportive, corrective feedback as a component of the monitoring function. By attending policy-planning meetings aimed at addressing particular issues, team members provided information about how other courts successfully resolved similar problems and provided appropriate research on the issue.

Advocacy

The empowerment model discourages evaluators from advocating for members within a team or group—instead, it encourages members to work toward collective solutions. However, evaluators may serve as direct advocates in the group process in a larger social context. This can be accomplished by taking collective decisions on policy issues and testifying before lawmakers, writing grants, and perhaps most important, writing in "public arenas to change public opinions, influence power brokers, and provide relevant information at opportune moments in the policy decision-making forum" (Fetterman, Kaftarian, and Wandersman, 1996, p. 14).

The OSSRD has provided information advocating for the development of drug courts to the state legislature, and has worked to develop new courts by providing assistance in writing grants to implement or enhance existing drug courts. The evaluators, rather than individual team members, advocate for the drug court programs and processes.

Illumination

Illumination is the process whereby new insights and understanding take place as the result of a coordinated group effort. Once this occurs, team members are able to ask questions that can be answered through additional research.

The OSSRD team has gleaned information about drug court functioning as well as program outcomes by monitoring program activities and facilitating the problem-solving process. This information is valuable to drug court professionals as they attempt to plan and implement programs. One example is the importance of establishing the judge as the team leader early in the process.

Liberation

The final step in the process occurs when team members, armed with knowledge concerning program strengths and weaknesses, find new ways to build on those successes and failures. They discover new ways to evaluate their own progress—liberating them from old roles and limitations.

Liberation will result when the courts are fully functioning, have internalized the evaluation process, and have the ability to identify their own training needs. Some courts in Louisiana have taken evaluation results and restructured parts of their program. Innovative treatment programs, such as gender-specific groups, have been developed because the evaluation identified a disproportionate loss of minority clients. Gender-specific groups have been developed because the evaluation identified under-represented female participants with unique treatment issues. Minority-specific groups grew out of the need to provide culturally sensitive and specific materials to minority clients, as the evaluation results found that programs had difficulty retaining that population. Evaluation can be the catalyst for self-evaluation, which both validates strengths and challenges weaknesses.

Steps of Empowerment Evaluation

The first step in empowerment evaluation involves taking stock of the program. Team members rate the current program's components on a 1 to 10 scale, and document its effectiveness. This information provides a baseline to measure future success. In the second step, team members are asked to determine the type of rating the program should receive in the future. They develop a set of goals that will help them attain that future rating. Based on critical reviews and consensual agreement among team members, objectives are created to detail how those goals will be attained. For the third step, the group develops a set of strategies that can be used to accomplish program objectives. These strategies are continually reviewed to determine their effectiveness. The final step calls for team members to determine the type of documentation necessary to monitor progress toward their goals. Team members must explain how each type of documentation is relevant to measuring program goals so that they do not gather information that is not useful or not relevant to the process.

Limitations

No evaluative technique is without limitations. Several issues have been raised concerning empowerment evaluation, including lack of research rigor when compared to traditional evaluation, maintaining objectivity, and participant and program bias. Balance and flexibility are key components of empowerment evaluation, which is not meant to supplant the use of traditional evaluation but is designed to address a specific evaluative need. Objectivity is an ongoing issue for a drug court evaluation team. Rigorous self-examination and adhering to objectives and protocols are checks that can be employed by the team to reduce bias. This requires critical analysis, cooperation, communication, and self-reflection.

Conclusion

This new evaluation approach has been used in a wide variety of arenas including health, mental health, criminal justice, and in the educational system ranging from preschool to doctoral programs. A great number of programs have successfully incorporated this model into their evaluations; however, its developer is quick to remind followers (and in an attempt to quiet critics), that it is not a panacea, and should not be used to replace other forms of evaluation. The approach continues to evolve, and there is still much to learn.

REFERENCES

Bandura, A. (1982). Self-efficacy mechanism in human agency. *American Psychologist, 37*(2), 122-147.

Fetterman, D.M., Kaftarian, S.J., and Wandersman, A. (Eds.) (1996). *Empowerment evaluation knowledge and tools for self-assessment and accountability.* Thousand Oaks, CA: Sage.

Hellriegal, D., Slocum, J.W., and Woodman, R.W. (1995). *Organizational behavior.* New York: West.

Office of Justice Programs: Summary of Drug Court Activity (February 2000). Drug Court Technical Assistance Project. Washington, DC: American University.

Oja, S.N. and Smulyan, L. (1989). *Collaborative action research.* Philadelphia: Falmer.

Papineau, K. and Kiely, M.C. (1994). Participatory evaluation: Empowering stakeholders in a community economic development organization. *Community Psychologist, 27(2),* 56-57.

Rappaport, J. (1987). Terms of empowerment/exemplars of prevention: Toward a theory for community psychology. *American Journal of Community Psychology, 15*(April), 121-148.

Reason, P. (Ed.) (1988). *Human inquiry in action: Developments in new paradigm research.* Newbury Park, CA: Sage.

Tax, S. (1996). The Fox Project. *Human Organization, 17,* 17-19. In D.M. Fetterman, S.J. Kaftarian, and A. Wandersman (Eds.), *Empowerment evaluation knowledge and tools for self-assessment and accountability.* Thousand Oaks, CA: Sage.

Tuckman, B.W., and Jensen, M.A. (1977). Stages of small-group development revisited. *Group and Organizational Studies 2*(4), 419-427.

Whitmore, E. (1990). Empowerment in program evaluation: A case example. *Canada Social Work Review, 7*(2), 215-229.

Whyte, W.F. (Ed.) (1990). *Participatory action research.* Newbury Park, CA: Sage.

Zimmerman, M.A. (1987). Empowerment theory: Psychological, organizational, and community levels of analysis. In J. Rappaport and E. Seldman (Eds.), *Handbook of community psychology* (p. 725). New York: Plenum.

Chapter 6

Is Social Work Y2K Compliant? Adapting to the Mandates of Future Practice

Jacquelyn Mitchell

INTRODUCTION

Social workers joined the world in a collective sigh of relief on the first business day of the year 2000. The dreaded "millennium bug" had raised anxieties that automated data and data systems would be destroyed. The world was sent scurrying to institute preventive measures. However, the nail biting proved overreactive, as the entry of the year 2000 was anticlimatic. "Nothing special happened" despite the "hype and scattered hysteria" ("Millennium bug doesn't bite," 2000; Smith, W. C., citing Douglas E. Phillips, 2000, p. 88).

Perhaps the relief will be short-lived. Perhaps there is also merit to the suggestion that the real Y2K crisis is about more than computer glitches, and that future repercussions might be more awesome than the experience of simply stepping into 2000. Averting the technological scare might ultimately be dwarfed by other potential rigors imbedded in the new millennium (Smith, W. C., 2000; Williamson, 2000).

Some lingering exigencies peculiar to the year 2000 still exist. Lawsuits have been filed against various players in the software industry (Smith, W. C., 2000). Congressional investigations have been launched into the lessons learned, the costs associated with the lessons, and whether the costs were justified (Horn, 2000). Challenges that were emerging pre-year 2000 continue; human poverty and inequality persistently increase globally (Williamson, 2000) amid the development of global "e-commerce" (Smith, D., 2000).

Relative to the future of social work, forecasts are diverse. Some warn of the potential end of the profession based on the obsolescence of extant social work interventions, the obsolescence of the profession's philosophical and value-based orientation, and changes in the social structure precipitated by marketplace dynamics (Kreuger, 1997). On the other hand, the historical resiliency and capacity of social work have been offered as a forecast of future success for the profession (Gibelman, 1999). A future shaped by changes reverberating within host settings and society generally has also been predicted (Franklin, 2000).

Such forecasting is a delicate and inexact endeavor. The certainty of such predictions is not guaranteed. Nonetheless, contemplating the "immediate future" in preparation for future challenges "is important for thriving in an environment of change" (Franklin, 2000, p. 5).

In preparation for future challenges, the technologically based fears the social work profession shared with the rest of the world on the eve of the year 2000 might not be pivotal. Instead, the less technological demands that accompany the entry into the new millennium might be more critical to determining whether social work can survive and thrive in the future. It is within that context that the Y2K readiness of social work is explored.

This chapter focuses on one set of potential challenges for social work and social workers in the new century: welcome and unwelcome mandates that may govern the profession and practitioners. Though often external to the profession and the profession's influence, these edicts seem poised to significantly shape social work and social workers. Perhaps it is no longer a question of whether social workers will be faced with these mandates, but whether they and the profession can successfully accommodate these mandates now and in the future (Swenson, 1993; Saltzman and Furman, 1999).

For purposes of this discussion, the term "mandate" refers to any of the defining dictates that emanate from "the law," the complex system of processes, procedures, and rules of social control that are derived from the various constitutions, statutes, rules, regulations, principles, and precedents that are adopted, administered, and enforced by the authority of law and the resultant bureaucratic structure. These mandates emerge from various sources (e.g., legislation, rules and regulations, and case law) and provide the underlying authority for other prescriptions, such as nonprofit organizational status, social work licensure, social work professional status, and social work services (Lynch and Mitchell, 1992).

The discussion here is intended to be proactive, rather than infallibly predictive. Moreover, the perspective is multifaceted and addresses the proliferation of mandates emanating from the profession, licensure boards, the law and the courts, and workplace prescriptions that are shaping social work practice as the profession moves into its second century and the new millennium.

The chapter begins with a discussion of the contexts and dimensions of social work practice, including historical and future perspectives. The discussion then turns to the "good" mandates that are welcomed by the profession as compatible with a vibrant and strong future for social work and social workers. The exploration of the "bad" mandates (i.e., those perceived as less compatible and more threatening to the future of the social work profession, as we know it) follows. Consideration is then focused on readiness for practice in the future, including implications for social work, social workers, social work practice, and social work education.

EVOLUTION TO THE FUTURE: THE CONTEXT AND DIMENSIONS OF SOCIAL WORK PRACTICE

The contextual mosaic within which Y2K readiness of social work is addressed is significantly shaped by the profession's response to similar mandates over its one-hundred-year history. The current relationship between social work and the law, and the contemporary status of the social work profession contribute to the perspective of the discussion.

In the social work profession, discussions of mandates tend to predominantly focus externally, licensure being a notable exception. This tendency toward external focus may be a reflection of what social workers are taught, as such a bias is evident in social work curricula relative to content that incorporates the mandates discussed here. For example, social work students in accredited programs are required to take a foundation course on social welfare policy, content that is thought to contribute to distinguishing social work from other professions. However, as Ginsberg (1998) notes, these courses tend to give short shrift to mandates that directly impact social work and social workers. Instead, they are framed from the perspective of policy as "the primary underpinning of *social programs*" related to client systems (p. 11, emphasis added).

Interestingly, pioneers such as Sophonisba Breckinridge, advocated for course offerings on social work and the law. Social work programs eventually moved toward the inclusion of such content. Yet these courses have also tended to be both "other" directed and isolated within curricula, with little attention to the regulation of social work practice and social workers or the relevance of the content across curricula (Barker and Branson, 1993).

Minor exceptions are reflected in social work practice in settings related to the courts and corrections. In such instances in which the realities of contemporary practice require interface with the law, social workers give some attention to the associated mandates. Nonetheless, as a general notion, the profession continues to be disinclined toward and to rebuff anything "legalistic" (Barker and Branson, 1993, p. 6), and to exhibit "legist phobia," an anxiety caused by interfacing with systems involving the law (Lynch and Mitchell, 1995b, p. 10).

Notably, this contemporary landscape does not reflect the historical evidence of the partnership between social work and law. Even though nineteenth-century social workers were "probation officers" in juvenile courts and shared memberships with attorneys in professional associations, such a partnership seems an unlikely scenario from the perspective of the year 2000. Although the two professions continue to share client systems, because clients with social problems often also have legal problems, the historical interdependence of the two disciplines has significantly waned (Lynch and Mitchell, 1992; Barker and Branson, 1993).

The divorce of the two disciplines remains inchoate. Faint voices from the legal side acknowledge the value of social work skills to "get to the root causes," to "solve related difficulties of the whole person," and to provide "continuing help" relative to matters brought to the courts (Weinstein, 1999, p. 391). Some social work commentators have also encouraged acknowledgment and exploitation of the potential value of social work skills to the American judicial system (Lynch and Mitchell, 1995a; Barker and Branson, 1993). However, these views do not represent the majority in either profession (Lynch and Mitchell, 1995a).

A final piece of the contextual mosaic against which this discussion proceeds involves contemporary perspectives on the social work profession. The primary mission of the profession is to "enhance human well-being and help meet the basic needs of all people, with particular attention to the needs and empowerment of people who are vulnerable, oppressed, and living in poverty." The mission is actualized through the promotion of social justice and social change, and is premised on six related core values, including the core value of competence (NASW, 1996, p. 1). Perspectives on the potential post-Y2K maintenance of this mission vary. Some commentators have projected an optimistic future from the vantage point of the 100th anniversary of the profession (Gibelman, 1999), suggesting, for example, that social workers will have the influence necessary to "shape the future" (Allen-Meares, 1997, p. 432). However, others have suggested that social work is in need of a substantial overhaul to better cope with the present and to prepare for the future (Bisno and Cox, 1997; Epstein, 1992).

This is the context within which the question is asked: "Is social work Y2K ready?" In other words, is social work ready to respond to and practice within a changing environment? Are social work and social workers prepared to survive and thrive in a society in which litigiousness and regulations dictate practice settings, practice expertise, and educational prerequisites? Are social work and social workers prepared to accommodate and benefit from the "good" and the "bad" mandates of Y2K and beyond?

On the "Good" Mandates

Some mandates under which social workers practice have the potential to enhance the stature of the profession. Notable mandates are those that are promulgated by social work professional associations, such as the National Association of Social Workers (NASW), and the Council on Social Work Education (CSWE). Through its *Code of Ethics* (1996), peer review-based adjudication processes, and credentialing programs, NASW regulates the practice conduct of practitioners who are association members (NASW, 1996; NASW, 1999; Barker and Branson, 1993). Self-regulation in the area of social work education is under the aegis of CSWE (CSWE, 1999a; CSWE, 1999b).*

CSWE (1994a,b) accreditation standards are envisioned as establishing minimal requirements. The standards function as a vehicle through which social work education programs are certified as "having a level of performance, integrity, and quality that entitles them to the confidence of the educational community and the public they serve" (p. 1). Through the accreditation process, social work educators prescribe the knowledge and skills the social work profession considers essential to guide the educational preparation of future practitioners (Drolen, 1999).

In combination, these mandates are viewed as contributing to the status of the social work profession and, therefore, social workers. Significantly, the NASW *Code of Ethics* (1996), and the CSWE-led effort toward institutionalization of social work knowledge standards (CSWE, 1994a; CSWE, 1994b) exemplify three of the elements of professionalism under the classic analysis of Ernest Greenwood (1957)—that is, a professional code of conduct, systematic theory, and professional culture.

---

*CSWE has established accreditation standards for baccalaureate and master's level programs. For purposes of the discussion here, the standards will be referenced collectively.

Licensing statutes, a third source of mandates, are a "mixed bag" relative to characterization as profession "enhancing" or profession "constricting." Support for these mandates within the profession suggests the profession-enhancing aspects of social work licensure. However, social work licensure is overseen by boards that are politically appointed and that prioritize protection of the public, as opposed to enhancement of professional stature. Nonetheless, in some quarters of the profession, licensure statutes are applauded as having the potential to "bring about better and more effective help for the clients of social workers," a result that "can only be good for the client, the social work profession, and society!" (Karls, 1992, p. 65).

Clearly, as a result of licensure, social workers have gained varying degrees of professional benefit—from title protection to third-party vendor status (Saltzman and Furman, 1999; Barker and Branson, 1993). The social work profession has also benefitted from mandates generated by other statutory and regulatory schema that define the public and private workplace. Contractual protections and perquisites are among those rewards. Legal mandates have conferred and affirmed licensure and professional status for social work, supporting vendorship and other career opportunities for social workers (Barker and Branson, 1993; Saltzman and Furman, 1999; Mitchell and Lynch, 1997).

The judicial system is yet another source of "good" mandates that affect the social work profession. For example, the professional stature and autonomy of social work was bolstered by judicial confirmation of the profession's authority to self-regulate via enforcement of the *Code* through the NASW adjudicatory processes (*Neumark v. National Association of Social Workers, Inc.*, 762 F 2d 993 (1985); NASW, 1999; NASW, 1991). Courts also tend to turn to ethical codes to establish a standard of care in matters involving professional conduct (Constantinides, 1991).

The U.S. Supreme Court decision in *Jaffe v. Redmond,* 518 U.S. 1 (1996), is an additional example of a "good," judicially afforded mandate. Noting that the legislatures in forty-six states had mandated a testimonial privilege for licensed social workers, the *Jaffe* court case held that the privilege was also applicable to clinical social workers in federal courts, pursuant to Rule 501 of the *Federal Rules of Evidence.* In dicta, the court also indirectly recognized the expertise of social workers as parallel to that of psychiatrists and psychologists, reinforcing the role of social workers as expert witnesses as advanced by other commentators (see e.g., Gothard, 1989; Barker and Branson, 1993; Lynch and Mitchell, 1995a; Saltzman and Furman, 1999).

These are some of the mandates imbedded in the changing landscape of the new millennium that have been generally encouraged and welcomed by social work and social workers. They are sources of potential professional and personal benefits for the profession and practitioners in the twenty-first century and beyond. However, realizing the benefit of these legally generated rewards, benefits, and protections, and handling possible less "social-work friendly" side effects are dependent upon the Y2K readiness of social work and social workers (Barker and Branson, 1993; Lynch and Mitchell, 1995a).

MANDATES AS "BAD THINGS"

Given the complexity of the law in its various forms and permutations, the "good" mandates discussed can have profession "constricting" side effects that are not so "social-work friendly." Indeed, in some respects, the "bad" mandates discussed at this point are, in many respects, essentially the flip side of the preceding discussion of the "good" mandates. The various legally sanctioned benefits also present new challenges, as may be evident in any contemporary setting or workplace. Regulatory complexity, compressed client services, varied and frequent malpractice claims, and other practice restrictions are frequently encountered by contemporary social work practitioners (Barker and Branson, 1993; Mitchell and Lynch, 1997).

For example, the autonomy to self-regulate utilizing the NASW *Code of Ethics,* peer-review procedures, and credentialing programs is not isolated from outside influences. The NASW adjudicatory process is subject to judicial review. As a result, the judicial power through which the vitality of the adjudicatory procedures was confirmed also serves as the ultimate review authority relative to the implementation of those procedures. Moreover, the judicial affirmation of self-regulation via the *Code,* and the NASW procedures brought increased practitioner responsibilities to be aware of (*Neumark v. National Association of Social Workers, Inc.,* 762 F2d 993 (1985); NASW, 1991; NASW, 1999; Mitchell and Lynch, 1997).

Significantly, the *Code* incorporates the duality evident in the relationship between self-regulation and the law. The practice standards contained in the *Code* variously prescribe practitioner conduct relative to the law as a potential practice resource, as well as a regulator of practice. For example, social work practitioners are variously urged to avoid violations of the civil or legal rights of clients, to advocate for policy and legislative changes, and to protect the rights of those adjudicated legally incompetent. Failure to exercise these multiple professional responsibilities can provide the basis for adjudication through the peer review process. As noted, the results of the peer process may be subject to judicial review (*Shapiro v. Butterfield,* 921 SW2d 649 (1996); *Neumark v. National Association of Social Workers, Inc.,* 762 F2d 993 (1985); Mitchell and Lynch, 1997; NASW, 1991).

The profession's autonomy in the area of the regulation of social work education is, likewise, limited. Social work educators are becoming aware that legal mandates have encroached into the "halls of ivy." For example, Cole and Lewis (1993) have noted that "legal issues" accompany the responsibility of social work educators to execute the "gate-keeping" function of graduating "professionals who are academically, behaviorally, and ethically suited to practice" (p. 1). They further conclude, after exploring several cases on the subject, that the "strongest recommendation that can be offered in relation to both conduct and disabling decisions is for program administrators to seek university counsel while developing rules of conduct and before taking adverse action" (p. 9).

Similarly, the benefits of social work licensure are accompanied by the responsibilities of licensure, notably, being subject to oversight boards. The American Association of State Social Work Boards (AASSWB),* the association of these oversight boards, has published a model practice act that offers a glimpse of the potential parameters of this oversight in the new millennium. In addition to mandating the professional conduct of licensed practitioners, the model act may also serve to erode the professional autonomy exercised by NASW and CSWE (AASSWB, 1997).

In introductory comments on the model act, AASSWB (1997, p. 4) noted that the standards of practice and educational requirements do not incorporate the NASW *Code of Ethics* (1996), or require that social workers possess a degree from a social work education program accredited by CSWE (CSWE 1994a,b). This decision is reportedly based upon the "risk" of regulatory boards being "accused of unlawfully delegating authority" and "an acknowledgment of the valid differences that exist between professional associations and professional regulatory boards":

> A professional organization's code of ethics is aspirational and voluntary. These characteristics are extremely well-suited to the mission of a professional association, but potentially problematic for regulatory boards, which have to develop statutes and regulations that are *legally enforceable.* (p. 4, emphasis added)

Thus, the licensure statutes, as presently formulated and as proposed for the future, may not totally be "a good thing" for the profession, in their own right and/or in combination with the NASW adjudication process (Barker and Branson, 1993; Saltzman and Furman, 1999). The regulatory schema advanced by the AASSWB (1997) model practice act suggests the potential of future dissonance with the interests of the social work profession.

---

*AASSWB recently changed its name to the "Association of Social Work Boards," to be more inclusive and more accurately reflect the membership of boards in Washington, DC, the U.S. Virgin Islands, and Alberta, Canada ("Social work boards' group changes name," 2000).

It is, perhaps, equally significant that internal and external mandates can currently operate to result in multiple exposures of social workers to sanctions. For example, licensing boards' disciplinary processes often include referral of findings of violation to NASW. NASW may also make such referrals to licensing boards, and the referrals may be further repeated to other professional associations in which a social worker might hold membership (Barker and Branson, 1993; Saltzman and Furman, 1999). Ultimately, either mandate might serve as the basis for the imposition of civil and/or criminal liability (Mitchell and Lynch, 1997; Saltzman and Furman, 1999; Barker and Branson, 1993). The stakes for licensed practitioners might be raised if the AASSWB (1997) model practice act is adopted by a significant number of jurisdictions. Repercussions could be seen throughout the entire regulatory schema emanating from internal and external sources (Biggerstaff, 2000; Mitchell and Lynch, 1997; AASSWB, 1997).

Parenthetically, licensure seems neither universally accepted by social workers nor guaranteed for the social work profession, suggesting further legal implications. Mathis (1992), for example, suggests social work licensure (1) "narrows the scope and the nature of services delivered to people of color and other disadvantaged communities"; (2) "restricts job opportunities for people of color"; and (3) utilizes "invalid and biased testing" and "university-based education" to restrict "the entry of people of color and unorthodox perspectives into the profession" (p. 59). This internal dissension is accompanied by recurring efforts essentially to reverse gains in the area of licensure by forces external to the social work profession. Recent action by the Idaho legislature is illustrative. That body acted to exempt medical facilities from the aegis of the social work practice act (O'Neill, 2000; Beacar, 2000).

Statutory mandates also proscribe social work practice and expose social workers and social work settings to sanctions. The Americans with Disabilities Act, P. L. 101-336, (ADA) is a notable example. As McEntee (1995) suggests, the client advocacy opportunities provided by statutes such as the ADA may collide with the accommodation and resource mandates that are imposed.

Social workers are statutorily required to report suspected abuse, on the pain of criminal penalty (Saltzman and Furman, 1999), and social work practice has been substantially shaped by the retrenchment of practice opportunities and autonomy that have accompanied the advent of managed care legislation (NASW, 1997; Sutter, 1998).

Indeed, depending upon practice settings, social workers might be subject to myriad legislative and regulatory mandates, varying from statutes designed to regulate procreation, prohibit discrimination, ensure rights in the health care arena, regulate the design of facilities, and/or secure confidentiality or other protections to specialized populations (see e.g., Saltzman and Furman, 1999; Multiethnic Placement Act of 1994, as amended, P. L. 103-382, P. L. 104-188; Alexander, 2000). Statutory and judicial influences are also transforming the role of social workers as expert witnesses. Licensure is often a condition precedent to acting as an expert (*Jaffe v. Redmond,* 518 U.S. 1 (1996); Biggerstaff, 2000). Furthermore, recent case law suggests that expert testimony will be more prescribed by courts and some professional societies to thwart "junk science" (Margulies, 1998). The U.S. Supreme Court's decision in *Daubert v. Merrell-Dow Pharmaceuticals, Inc.,* 509 U.S. 579 (1993) is illustrative.

The *Daubert* court introduced a new standard for the admissibility of expert testimony under the *Federal Rules of Evidence,* establishing a four-pronged test:

1. Whether the scientific theory or technique upon which the testimony is based has been validated as reliable
2. Whether the expert opinion has been subjected to peer review and publication
3. Whether the opinion is reliable—that is, based upon sound methodology
4. Whether the opinion has been accepted by the professional community of which the expert is a member

Although the *Daubert* expert was an epidemiologist, the applicability of the *Daubert* case to all expert testimony was established in *Kumho v. Carmichael,* 526 U.S. 137 (1999). As a result of *Daubert* and *Kumho,* social workers appearing as expert witnesses must be prepared for the evaluation of their testimony under a standard of "intellectual rigor" (*Kumho,* p. 1176).

Other areas of practice have been likewise proscribed by judicial mandates. For example, the California Supreme Court essentially reconstructed the NASW *Code of Ethics* (NASW, 1996) prescription to maintain confidentiality. In *Tarasoff v. Board of Regents of the University of California,* 551 P.2d 334 (1976), the court held that social workers have an absolute duty to warn of potential danger to others, notwithstanding professional confidentiality rules. Courts have also held social workers to standards of effective treatment (*Horak v. Biris,* 474 N.E. 2d 13, 1985), sexual misconduct (*Horak v. Biris,* 474 N.E. 2d 13, 1985; *Simmons v. United States of America,* 805 F.2d 1363, 1986), and breach of contract (*Martino v. Family Service Agency of Adams County,* 445 N.E. 2d 6, 1982). *DeShaney v. Winnebago County Department of Social Service,* 489 U.S. 189 (1989) left open the question of the extent to which social workers in public settings may be subject to liability for constitutional deprivation. It based its decision on the fact that the social workers in that instance were not liable for damages on a Section 1983 claim on the peculiar facts of the case before it.

These are some of the mandates on the darker side of the context within which to question whether social work is Y2K ready. Is it ready to respond to, practice within, and advocate for clients within the strictures that emanate from the mandates of practice in the twenty-first century and beyond? Are social work and social workers prepared to survive and thrive in a society in which litigiousness and regulation dictate practice settings and practice expertise? Can the social work profession and its mission to promote social justice and social change be preserved within the context of the new millennium?

ON FUTURE READINESS AND IMPLICATIONS FOR SOCIAL WORK PRACTICE AND EDUCATION

Because of the difficulty and inexactness of future forecasting (Franklin, 2000), the question of Y2K readiness of social work recurs. However, the efficacy of the inquiry is suggested by the essentiality of accommodating twenty-first century challenges within the context of the mission of social work practice. In the final analysis, the responsive discussion must incorporate considerations of the potential benefits, the challenges, and the opportunities of the future for social work practice and education. Moreover, the analysis must be considered within the context of the mission of the profession (i.e., social justice and social change) and, therefore, the profession itself (Specht and Courtney, 1994; Haynes and White, 1999).

Given the totality of the circumstances, the most sagacious response to the inquiry of the Y2K readiness of social work and social work practitioner is tentative. However, the transformation to a state of readiness is not impossible.

To be prepared for the new frontiers of the twenty-first century and beyond, the social work profession must provide practitioners, students, and educators with the resources with which to survive and thrive in an environment of change (Franklin, 2000). Because the change context is significantly defined by "legalistic" mandates (Barker and Branson, 1993), the response must reflect those idiosyncrasies.

Preparedness will require social workers to be legally literate in the mandates that impact clients, the profession, and practitioners (Lynch and Mitchell, 1995b; Saltzman and Furman, 1999; Barker and Branson, 1993). If the profession and its mission are to be sustained, social workers must be prepared to practice and promote social justice and change within the context created by the mandates that directly legislate social work practice and the social work practitioner (Mitchell and Lynch, 1997; Saltzman and Furman, 1999; *Gersch v. Illinois Department of Professional Rehabilita-*

tion, et al., 308 Ill. App. 3rd 649, 1999; *Jaffe v. Redmond,* 518 U.S. 1, 1996).

Perhaps social workers practicing in "legally related" settings can inform the definition and acquisition of the legal literacy required for the year 2000 and beyond. In response to a survey, a sample of NASW members whose primary and/or secondary practice setting was "legally related" suggest the following requisites:

1. Knowledge of the law, legal processes, and procedures that impact practice
2. Inclusion of content on law, and legal processes and procedures in MSW and BSW curricula
3. Inclusion of content related to law and legal processes and procedures in continuing education, conference, and on-the-job training offerings
4. Development of practice resources that include content on the law and legal processes and procedures
5. Expansion of the attention of professional social work associations to content on law and legal processes and procedures, including the development of practice sections (Mitchell and Lynch, 1998)

Commentators have espoused the need for similar resources. It has been suggested, for example, that the profession is yet to actively acknowledge either the potentially coercive or potentially beneficent characteristics of the mandates that shape social work practice. Little evidence that the profession generally sees the benefits of more "legally related" training or the potential of additional practice opportunities in "legally related" settings exists. In other words, social work and social workers do not yet seem prepared to exploit the legally generated and complex benefits and protections, or to prophylactically plan toward averting the potential detriments of the "bad" mandates (Barker and Branson, 1993; Lynch and Mitchell, 1995a).

Preparedness for the new millennium and beyond should not be allowed to be constrained by the "inertia of tradition" that constricts prioritization of other than mental health-related content in curricula and continuing education (Bisno and Cox, 1997, p. 384). Indeed, providing opportunities for knowledge augmentation related to the law and legal processes and procedures through curricular offerings, conference presentations, and practice resources, is essential to the development of the legal literacy suggested here as requisite to Y2K readiness (Barker and Branson, 1993; Lynch and Mitchell, 1995a; Saltzman and Furman, 1999).

Models for such an undertaking have been advanced. For example, Kopels and Gustavsson (1996) have suggested that instruction on legal issues should be infused across social work curricula. Lynch and Mitchell (1995a) offer a model for developing a "judicial social worker" specialty and for augmenting existing social work curricula and practice resources with instruction on legal theory, process, and procedure adequate to support effective social work practice in the twenty-first century and beyond.

Although the model chosen to prepare students and practitioners can, perhaps, best be determined through exercise of the collective wisdom of the profession, such preparation is an essential piece of the groundwork for Y2K readiness. Readiness depends on reconnecting the talk of practice competence—a core values of social work—with the realities of the context within which the profession exists and practitioners practice. Indeed, we are facing a new millennium, a second century of social work practice, and the blurring of national boundaries. If social workers are currently without the tools to engage a national social justice agenda, how can social justice be preserved as one of social work's grand traditions within the global context of the future? (Kreuger, 1997; Bisno and Cox, 1997).

Moreover, an earlier observation by Lynch and Mitchell (1992) underscores the efficacy of Y2K readiness of social work to thrive and survive within the playing field of existing and expanding "legally related" mandates. They suggest these mandates also create "a new practice frontier," a "wealth of current and future social work practice opportunities, the actualization of which await remedial response to social workers' limited knowledge of the legal system and the restricted curricula of schools of social work" (p. 82).

The profession, practitioners, and educators are urged to respond to the requisite of legal literacy as one of the key elements to the preservation of the profession and its mission in the new millennium. The collective profession—practitioners, educators, and professional association—must meet the challenge of ensuring the legal literacy requisite to surviving and thriving in the twenty-first century and beyond, if social work is not to "become the profession formerly known as social work" (Haynes and White, 1999, p. 390).

REFERENCES

Alexander, Jr., R. (2000). *Counseling, treatment, and intervention: Methods with juvenile and adult offenders*. Belmont, CA: Brooks/Cole.

Allen-Meares, P. (1997). Using the lessons from our past in the future [editorial]. *Journal of Social Work Education, 33*(3), 430-432.

American Association of State Social Work Boards (1997). *Model practice act.* Available online: <http://www.aasswb.org/>.

Barker, R.L. and Branson, D.M. (1993). *Forensic social work: Legal aspects of professional practice.* Binghamton, NY: The Haworth Press.

Beacar, K.O. (2000). Licensing a mixed bag in >99. *NASW News, 45(*2), 9.

Biggerstaff, M.A. (2000). A critique of the model state social work practice act. *Social Work, 45*(2), 105-115.

Bisno, H. and Cox, F. (1997). Social work education: Catching up with the present and the future. *Journal of Social Work Education, 33*(2), 373-387.

Cole, B.S. and Lewis, R.G. (1993). Gatekeeping through termination of unsuitable social work students: Legal issues and guidelines. *Journal of Social Work Education, 29*(2), 150-160. Available online: <http://ehostvgw13.e>.

Constantinides, C. (1991). Professional ethics codes in court: Redefining the social contract between the public and the professions. *25 Georgia Law Review* 1327.

Council on Social Work Education (1994a). Curriculum policy statement for master's degree programs in social work education. Available online: <http://www.cswe.org/mswcps.htm>.

Council on Social Work Education (1994b). Curriculum policy statement for baccalaureate degree programs in social work education. Available online: <http://www.cswe.org/bswcps.htm>.

Daubert v. Merrell-Dow Pharmaceuticals, Inc., 509 U.S. 579 (1993).

DeShaney v. Winnebago County Department of Social Service, 489 U.S. 189 (1989).

Drolen, C.S. (1999). Do accreditation requirements deter curriculum innovation? No! *Journal of Social Work Education, 35*(2), 189-192.

Franklin, C. (2000). Predicting the future of school social work practice in the new millennium [editorial]. *Social Work in Education, 22*(1), 5-7.

Gersch v. Illinois Department of Professional Rehabilitation, et al., 308 Ill. App. 3rd 649 (1999).

Gibelman, M. (1999). The search for identity: Defining social work—Past, present, future. *Social Work, 44*(4), 298-310.

Ginsberg, L. (1998). *Conservative social welfare policy: A description and analyses.* Chicago: Nelson-Hall.

Gothard, S. (1989). Power in the court: The social worker as an expert witness. *Social Work, 34*(1), 65-67.

Greenwood, E. (1957). Attributes of a profession. *Social Work, 2,* 45-55.

Haynes, D.T. and White, B.W. (1999). Will the "real" social work please stand up? A call to stand for professional unity. *Social Work, 44*(4), 385-391.

Horak v. Biris, 474 N.E. 2d 13 (1985).

Horn, S. (2000). Was Y2K cost justified*? FDCH Congressional Testimony.* January 27.

Jaffe v. Redmond, 518 U.S. 1 (1996).

Karls, J.M. (1992). Should social workers be licensed? Rejoinder to Professor Mathis. In E. Gambrill and R. Pruger (Eds.), *Controversial issues in social work* (pp. 64-65). Boston: Allyn & Bacon.

Kopels, S. and Gustavsson, N.S. (1996). Infusing legal issues into the social work curriculum. *Journal of Social Work Education, 32*(1), 115-125.

Kreuger, L.W. (1997). The end of social work. *The Journal of Social Work Education, 33*(1), 19-27.

Kumho v. Carmichael, 526 U.S. 137 (1999).

Lynch, R.S. and Mitchell, J. (1992). Institutionalizing the roles of court social workers. *Journal of Law and Social Work, 3,* 77-87.

Lynch, R.S. and Mitchell, J. (1995a). Judicial social worker practice model: Paradigm for a specialty and curricula enhancement. *Journal of Law and Social Work, 5*(1), 25-40.

Lynch, R.S. and Mitchell, J. (1995b). Justice system advocacy: A must for NASW and the social work community. *Social Work, 40*(1), 9-12.

Margulies, J.B. (1998). Professional societies can help rid courts of junk science. *Legal Backgrounder,* 13, 50. Available online: <http://web.lexis-nexis.com>.

Martino v. Family Service Agency of Adams County, 445 N.E. 2d 6 (1982).

Mathis, T.P. (1992). Should social workers be licensed? No. In E. Gambrill and R. Pruger (Eds.), *Controversial issues in social work* (pp. 58- 64). Boston: Allyn & Bacon.

"Millennium bug doesn't bite" (2000). *NASW News, 45*(2), 9.

Mitchell, J. and Lynch, R.S. (1997). Do the ethical standards of the profession carry a higher authority than the law? No. In E. Gambrill and R. Pruger (Eds.), *Controversial issues in social work ethics, values, and obligations* (pp. 131-135). Boston: Allyn & Bacon.

Mitchell, J. and Lynch, R.S. (1998). Voices and visions of judicial social workers: Building on almost a century of justice system practice. Unpublished manuscript.

Multiethnic Placement Act of 1994, as amended, P. L. 103-382, P. L. 104-188.

National Association of Social Workers (1991). *NASW procedures for the adjudication of grievances* (Third edition). Washington, DC: Author.

National Association of Social Workers (1996). *Code of ethics*. Washington, DC: Author.

National Association of Social Workers (1997). *Social workers, managed care and antitrust issues*. Washington, DC: Author.

Neumark v. National Association of Social Workers, Inc., 762 F2d 993 (1985).

O'Neill, J.V. (2000). Compliance in sight, Idaho legislators repeal licensing. *NASW News, 45*(4), 5.

Saltzman, A. and Furman, D.M. (1999). *Law in social work practice* (Second edition). Chicago: Nelson-Hall.

Shapiro v. Butterfield, 921 SW2d 649 (1996).

Simmons v. United States of America, 805 F.2d 1363 (1986).

Smith, D. (2000). Yes, there really is life after Y2K. *Internetweek, 803,* 23-27.

Smith, W.C. (2000). Big prep for Y2K: Who should pay? *ABA Journal, 86,* 88.

"Social work boards' group changes name" (2000). *NASW News, 45*(3), 13.

Specht, H. and Courtney, M. (1994). *Unfaithful angels: How social work has abandoned its mission.* New York: Free Press.

Sutter, A.B. (1998). Sounding board: Managed care, Part I. *NASW Newsletter: Georgia Chapter, 19*(5), 6-7.

Swenson, L.C. (1993). *Psychology and law for the helping professions.* Pacific Grove, CA: Brooks/Cole.

Tarasoff v. Board of Regents of the University of California, 551 P.2d 334 (1976).

Weinstein, J.B. (1999). Legal ethics: When is a social worker as well as a lawyer needed? *Journal of the Institute for the Study of Legal Ethics, 2,* 391-399.

Williamson, T. (2000). The real Y2K crisis. *Dollars and Sense, 227* (January/February), 1.

Chapter 7

Life or Death? Using Multidisciplinary Life History Research in Forensic Social Work

Cecile C. Guin
Thomas S. Merrill

LIFE HISTORY RESEARCH: AN OVERVIEW

Life history research is the empirical inquiry into the history of a person's life (that, for the purposes of this chapter) is facing a capital trial. That is, the questions guiding the research are derived from those domains that have been empirically linked to the development of criminal behavior. The issue of life histories has become important in capital trials because of recent statutory and case law and established legal theory that clearly describes the responsibility of the defense attorney to thoroughly investigate the client's life (Gary S. Goodpaster's article in Wheeler and Pearson, 1995).

Defense counsel has the responsibility to:

> Investigate the client's life history, and emotional and psychological make-up, as well as the substantive case and defenses. There must be an inquiry into the client's childhood upbringing, education, relationships, friendships, formative and traumatic experiences, personal psychology, and present feelings. (Goodpaster's article, p. 2, cited in Wheeler and Pearson, 1995)

Empirical support exists for the need to have comprehensive evaluations in criminal defense, an issue that is magnified with capital defense (Blume, 1995; Wagner, 1995). The authors, through their experience in various types of court evaluations and recommendations, propose that life history research can best be accomplished through the use of a multidisciplinary team approach. Depending on the specifics of the case, the defense counsel would identify a social worker and a psychologist to conduct the initial investigation and make recommendations for additional team members.

Life history research must begin with a thorough development of the defendant's life history, including social, educational, medical, criminal, economic, mental health, and family history. Figure 7.1 shows a theoretical approach to information-gathering by the social worker who is conducting the research (Guin, 1991). The collection of data in specific areas of investigation is empirically linked to substantiated findings regarding criminal development, and ongoing behavior. The initial life history report must be thorough so it can be passed on to the psychologist for a determination of the psychological aspects in the defendant's history. For example, based upon

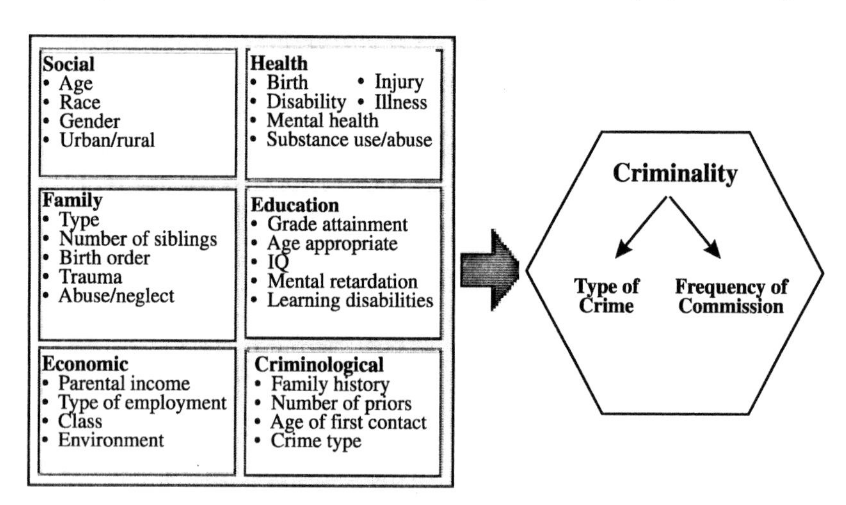

FIGURE 7.1. Factors to Examine Related to Criminal Development

school records and medical history, the psychologist can determine what type of intellectual assessment is needed and if there is a need to rule out injury from traumatic falls or head injuries. The psychologist can perform a battery of tests to gather more information, and make recommendations for psychiatric, medical, and neurological involvement. Through this initial team effort, the attorney can begin to integrate these findings with the facts of the case. For instance, perhaps the homicide was related to developmental disabilities that can explain how the defendant perceived the world at the time of the alleged crime. In another case, the incident may be related to domestic violence issues during the defendant's upbringing. Does identification of these types of issues require further expertise? Sometimes, the involvement of domestic violence counselors, experts in developmental disabilities, and/or experts in any area deemed relevant to the client's behavior at the time of the instant offense must be included in the team. Quite often, a neurologist or other medical expert is necessary to examine the client and to theorize earlier family history that has impacted the client.

The reason for the multidisciplinary effort is not to promote having five experts testify in a penalty phase or a sentencing hearing. Rather, the point of this research is to understand who the client is, so the life story can be effectively presented to the capital judge or jury. The "telling of the story" is the critical point of communication and must follow some type of integrated theory of how the client reached this point in his or her life. In some cases, an expert can guide this story or elaborate upon certain aspects of the story. Through life history research, the attorney, aided by a team, can determine who should convey the parts of the story—family members, neighbors, teachers, ministers, experts, etc. The intent is to create an accurate picture of the client and provide this information in a manner that can be understood by the judge and jury in order to make an informed decision.

The challenge to each of the contributing social disciplines is to examine traditional roles and responsibilities in the evaluation of offenders/clients, and redefine these roles as a multidisciplinary need. To serve the clients and the legal system in a responsible manner, each of the disciplines must add what they are best trained to contribute and recognize that the other disciplines also have a significant contribution to make.

TRADITIONAL ROLES IN SOCIAL WORK AND PSYCHOLOGY

The interface between social work and the law began as the earliest tenets of social work theory and development. In fact, early social workers were more involved with legal issues than mental or medical fields (Barker and Branson, 1993). In examining the beginnings of social work, the involvement of the profession in the legal system is demonstrated through work with abused children, the care of children, probation/parole, work with child labor laws, and involvement in the prison systems. Social workers have always assumed an advocacy role for their clients. This skill is required more in the courts than anywhere else, especially with indigent and disabled clients.

Society's poverty problems drew more social workers into that arena for many years, followed by an emphasis upon mental and medical health. From the 1930s to the 1950s, the profession focused on poverty issues. Then there was a shift toward involvement in mental health. Currently, there seems to be a gradual shift back to some of the more basic functions of the social work profession, including advocacy, community intervention, mediation, and case history documentation. Effective social work practice today requires client advocacy skills and knowledge of the legal system, regardless of the area of social practice being pursued. However, the practice of social work in legal settings is becoming more multidisciplinary in focus, and will require an interface with other professions involved in a particular case.

In traditional forensic social work practice, the social worker performs such functions as expert testimony, court evaluations, investigations of criminal conduct, sentencing recommendations, the monitoring and treatment of court-ordered clients, and mediation. This is in addition to the professional functions involved in development of licensing laws, and the provision of testimony in malpractice cases (Barker and Branson, 1993). In multidisciplinary forensic social work, the social worker may perform these functions, but it will be in the context of a team of professionals, each contributing their expertise from specific disciplines. The social worker may participate at various points in the development of the legal case. In capital trials, the social worker is generally the first point of contact for the development of the life history.

As a member of a multidisciplinary capital defense team, the social worker's role is tied to the development of factual mitigation evidence. Legal mitigation, depending on various state statutes, refers to the factual evidence that must be presented about a person when a jury is considering a life or death sentence. For example, in Louisiana, child abuse, mental retardation, mental illness, and coercive involvement in a crime are considered to be "mitigating factors." The jury is instructed to consider the presence of these factors in a defendant's life as plausible explanations for the commission of a crime. Often times, these factors are construed by the jury as "excuses." As a result, the link between the problem, the client's history, and the commission of the crime must be well-documented and described.

Mitigation evidence is derived from a thorough investigation into a person's life. This is the reason that social workers are so uniquely qualified for participating in capital trials. Graduate social work education and training prepare social workers to interview clients and family members, develop case histories and impartial documentation of life events, and, most important, to work with clients in their own environment. The social worker is trained to examine the "fit" between a person and his or her environment. As the social worker develops this history and identifies critical points in the development of a person, she or he can make recommendations to the defense attorney for appropriate additions to the professional team to develop a full life history.

The multidisciplinary team is critical to the defense of the capital client, not because of the issue of life or death, but because of the factual basis upon which that decision should be made. Criminal sentencing, especially in capital cases, must be based upon an accurate assessment of the client and a valid picture of who the client is. Capital jurors and judges can examine the legal issues with which they must deal to reach an honest verdict. In noncapital cases, juries and judges can make appropriate decisions as to the processing of the offender. The decision-making issues are diverse, but the point is to have a truthful foundation upon which a good decision can be made. With the complexity of human problems today, multidisciplinary teams are the only way to set the foundation for appropriate decisions.

When examining the traditional role of psychology, the foundation for psychology is clearly differentiated from the foundation of social work. Psychology is a data-driven discipline that developed out of empirical research. Psychology uses quantitative methods for normative-based evaluation, when necessary. With a high degree of reliability and validity, psychology can decide individual behavior. Psychologists often look at the population from which individual behaviors can be defined and determined.

The role of psychology in life history research is critical to a thorough understanding of the client. The social worker may tell the story of "how" a client reached a certain point in life—the psychologist provides the "why."

The practice of forensic psychology may be defined as "(1) the research endeavor that examines aspects of human behavior directly related to the legal process (e.g., eyewitness memory and testimony, jury decision making, or criminal behavior), and (2) the professional practice of psychology within or in consultation with a legal system that embraces both criminal and civil law" (Bartol and Bartol, 1987, p. 7).

By drawing on traditional psychological principles, the mitigation team can describe the client and his or her behavior with a high degree of certainty, validity, and reliability. The information can be presented to tell the defendant's story in a way that a jury may understand, and make sense of the defendant's behavior in the context of his or her entire life.

With these considerations in mind, the social work professional can play a critically important role in decision making in the legal system. As the first point of contact for legal hearings, the worker has the opportunity to use all of the skills of the social work profession to develop a thorough life history so that other professionals or experts quickly pinpoint the client's problem areas. The psychologist plays another critical role as they can conduct the assessments that will further pinpoint areas of concern. Together, the social worker and the psychologist can provide factual information on the life of the client and the cognitive attributes that underlie the life path taken.

One discipline cannot tell the client's story alone. The contributions of the psychologist are only as good as the life history development by the social worker. The assessment by a cultural expert or a domestic violence expert is only as accurate as the psychological evaluation and the factual presentation of life events. All of this work will lead to good decision making and effective teamwork when the various disciplines integrate their areas of expertise and work in a collaborative manner with the client, the family, and the attorney. Each team member has a unique role to play in the life history development, the identification of mitigation factors, and comprehensive understanding of who the client is and how he or she arrived at this point in his or her life.

DEMONSTRATION OF MULTIDISCIPLINARY WORK THROUGH TWO LIFE HISTORIES

The need for a multidisciplinary team is most evident when examining the characteristics of persons charged with and found guilty of capital crimes. Figures 7.2 and 7.3 provide two actual case examples of summary data gathered to present the life histories in two capital trials (BQ and JK). Through a review of these documents, the need for multidisciplinary involvement is clearly demonstrated. These cases were chosen because each case has a unique perspective to consider in the life development and the path that was taken that led to the commission of the crime.

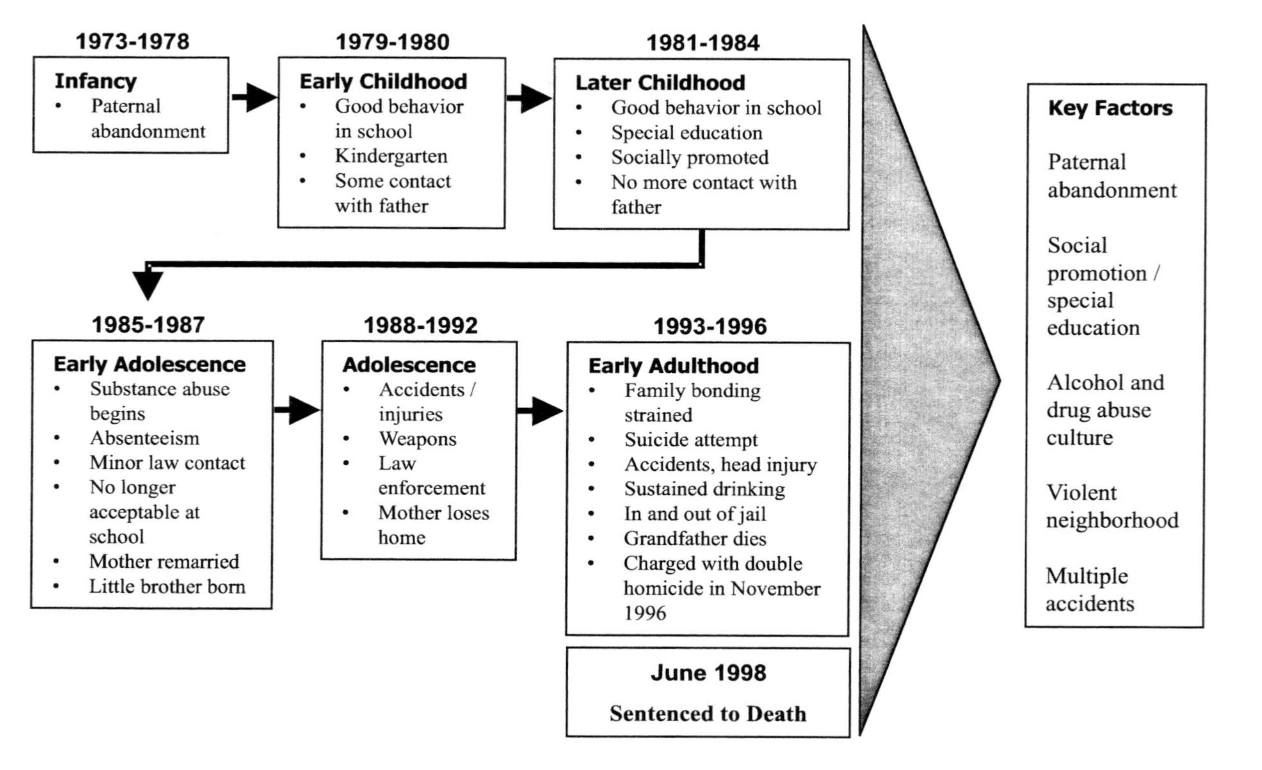

FIGURE 7.2. BQ—Development and Decline

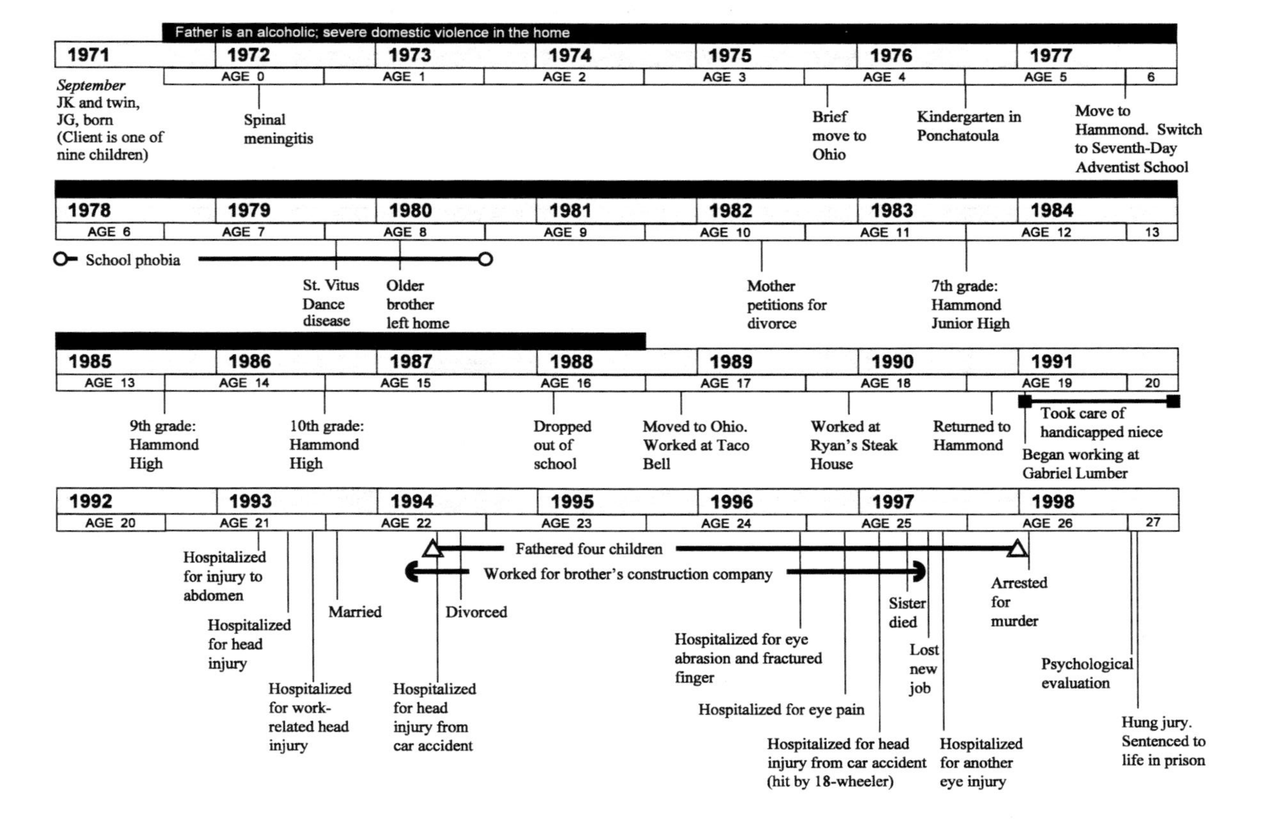

FIGURE 7.3. JK's Life Continuum

IMPLICATIONS FOR PRACTICE

The implications for social work and psychology are clear—the need for multidisciplinary action in developing the life history of a capital client is critical. Traditionally, each of the disciplines has taken an individualized approach to the development of historical information. This approach has been based upon the theoretical underpinnings of each of the professions. This will not serve the needs of the capital client. Capital clients often have multiple problems and multiple needs, both of which are exacerbated by the stress of a potential death penalty sentence. Complications within the client's family system are abundant and become an increasing problem as the capital trial date approaches. The multidisciplinary team member has an integral knowledge of these problems and can serve in an advocacy role for the client and his or her family most effectively.

The capital defense team must know their client from all perspectives in order to represent him or her effectively. Similarly, the jury deserves to have complete client information to make an informed decision about granting sentences of life or death.

Finally, a primary implication for practice is the plight of the victim and his or her family. The role of advocacy with an alleged offender is important, but no less important than the ethical responsibility to assist the victims of crime when appropriate and warranted.

As our culture becomes increasingly complex, our problems will also expand in complexity. There are no individualized explanations for criminal behavior. Multidisciplinary research and explanations for deviant behavior will become more important in our attempts to understand the criminal pathway. The field of forensic science is in a period of growth and progression. To become a part of that progress, social workers, psychologists, and other social sciences must reexamine traditional views and work toward the development of multidisciplinary teams for forensic work. In the case of capital clients, this collaborative work has become a necessity.

REFERENCES

Barker, R.L. and Branson, D.M. (1993). *Forensic Social Work.* Binghamton, NY: The Haworth Press.

Bartol, C.R. and Bartol, A.M. (1987). History of Forensic Psychology. In I.B. Weiner and A.K. Hess (Eds.), *Handbook of Forensic Psychology* (pp. 3-21). New York: John Wiley and Sons.

Blume, J. (1995). Mental Health Issues in Criminal Cases: The Elements of a Competent and Reliable Mental Health Examination. *The Advocate, 17*(4), 3-12.

Guin, C.C. (1991). "Juvenile to Adult Criminality in Louisiana." (University of Texas—Arlington), *Dissertation Abstracts International* AAG9131745.

Wagner, M.M. (1995). Neuro-Psychological Evidence in Criminal Defense: Rationale and Guidelines for Enlisting an Expert. *The Advocate, 17*(3), 8-11.

Wheeler, R.L. and Pearson, J. (1995). The Evidence of a Lifetime: Ignorance Is No Excuse. *The Advocate, 16*(6), 79-81.

Chapter 8

Psychological Testing for Social Workers in a Forensic Setting

Nina S. Broyles

INTRODUCTION

Harry Potter and Forensic Social Work

Who is Harry Potter and what does he have to do with social work in a forensic setting? Harry is the fictional hero of the books commonly known as the *Harry Potter* books. When the reader first meets Harry, he's an eleven-year-old who doesn't know who he is. Harry, like social workers in a forensic setting, is beginning a journey to an unfamiliar place to discover who he is. To get to this place, Harry must board the train at Platform 9 ¾. The problem is that there is no Platform 9 ¾. Harry knows that he must run toward the barricade between 9 and 10 and jump. With great faith, he leaps toward the barricade between the tracks and instead of crashing into the barricade, he finds himself on Platform 9 ¾, where a special train is waiting to take him to the Hogwarts School of Witchcraft and Wizardry. With a leap of faith, social workers too must move forward to break the barricade and become powerful and accurate witnesses in the forensic setting. We will do this without witchcraft or wizardry, but by learning what roles and skills are required of social workers in a forensic setting.

WHO ARE WE?

Although we are not psychologists, we are highly trained professionals with specialized skills, stated values, and a unique knowledge base. Because social workers work in the areas of juvenile justice, mediation, psychotherapy, social security, and disability in settings such as hospitals, courts, governmental agencies, and schools, the likelihood that social workers will be required to give expert or factual testimony in legal proceedings is great. The knowledge social workers gain in their contact with their clients can be valuable to courts. Psychological testing can provide a level of objectivity and accuracy that is often needed in the forensic setting.

Forensic testimony must not only be truthful but it must be objective. Objective and factual information is the lynchpin of effective testimony. Social workers must commit to learn as much as possible about all of the information available about clients, especially when called upon to testify in court.

WHAT DOES TESTING HAVE TO DO WITH IT?

Social workers' training does not historically include instruction in the administration, scoring, and interpretation of psychological tests. If we are to become forensic social workers, we cannot simply ignore the client's testing results. As social workers carefully read and study the test reports concerning clients, we will become familiar with the conclusions drawn by the examiner. We must then carefully compare our conclusions about the client with the conclusions of the examiner. If the testing data do not support our conclusions about the client, we should try to find out why. Discussion with the examiner or a trustworthy psychologist may help. The psychological evaluation may be an essential part of the client's profile; to ignore the results would be viewed by the courts as negatively impacting the social worker's credibility. On cross-examination, a social worker must be prepared to defend her or his conclusions, especially if there is a difference in the test result and her or his opinion.

A list of the more commonly used psychological tests follows. The list is a small fraction of the available tests but will be representative of those frequently used. These include intelligence and cognitive (verbal and nonverbal), achievement and basic skills, infant and early childhood, neuropsychology (language and memory), psychopathology and projective techniques, personality and temperament, behavior and health, vocational and counseling, and forensic tests.

COMMONLY USED TESTS

1. Intelligence and cognitive ability
   - Wechsler Adult Intelligence Scale (WAIS-III)
   - Wechsler Intelligence Scale for Children
2. Achievement and basic skills
   - Wechsler Individual Achievement Test (WIAT)
   - Wide Range Achievement Test (WRAT-3)
   - Test of academic performance
3. Infant and childhood development
   - Bayley Scales of Infant Development (BSID-II)
   - Boehm Test of Basic Concepts (Boehm-R)
   - Miller Assessment for Preschoolers (MAP)
4. Neuropsychological
   - NEPSY
   - Wechsler Memory Scale (WMS-III)
   - California Verbal Learning Test (CVLT)
5. Psychopathology and projective techniques
   - Beck Depression Inventory (BDI-II)
   - Children's Depression Inventory (CDI)
   - Personality Assessment Inventory (PAI)
   - Rorschach techniques
   - Substance Abuse Subtle Screening Inventory (SASSI)
   - MMPI

6. Behavior and health
   - Brown Attention-Deficit Disorder Scale
   - Conners' Rating Scales Revised
   - Adaptive Behavior Inventory for Children (ABIC)
7. Vocational and counseling
   - Career interest inventory
   - Wide Range Interest-Opinion
8. Forensic
   - Victoria Symptom Validity Test
   - Structured Interview of Reported Symptoms (SIRS)
   - Rogers Criminal Responsibility Assessment Scales (R-CRAS)

Because social workers have not traditionally been trained in the field of psychological testing, there are rules that social workers should follow when using psychological tests. These rules will ensure that the testimony given is effective and within the social workers' fields of expertise. The following rules apply to the use of all psychological tests.

THE FIVE COMMANDMENTS OF PSYCHOLOGICAL TESTING

Before Administering Any Test, Always Find Out If You Meet the Qualifications

Every testing source has qualifying requirements. These qualifications are generally published along with information about the test in the publisher's catalog. Typically, the ratings are A, B, or C. A "C" rating requires verification of a PhD-level degree in psychology or education or the equivalent in a related field, or verification of licensure or certification by an agency recognized by the publisher. The "B" level requires verification of a master's-level degree in psychology or education or the equivalent in a related field or verification of membership in, or certification by a professional association recognized by the publisher. Level "A" has no professional requirements, but adherence to the publisher's purchase and use policy is required. To qualify, one completes a written form found in every catalog.

Always Judge a Test's Usefulness by Three Criteria

The three criteria used to evaluate the quality of a psychological instrument are validity, reliability, and standardization. The validity of a test refers to its usefulness. The question that should be asked is "Does this test measure what it purports to measure?" If the test is used to measure an IQ, does it do that or does it measure vocational interests? If it measures vocational interests then it would not be a valid intelligence quotient.

Reliability is a measure of the consistency of the test. If the test were found to repeatedly result in the same kind of findings (IQ scores) then it would be said to be a reliable measure of intelligence.

Standardization is useful in making a determination about which specific group of people this measure will validly test. If a test to measure intelligence were given only to people on the Internet, then the test would be standardized only on people who have access to the Internet as opposed to the general population.

Test Results Alone Should **Never** *be Used to Make a* **Diagnosis**

A psychological test is only one measure of many that should be considered before making a diagnosis. Tests can predict the probability of success in an educational setting but cannot predict a will to succeed, desire to perform, or commitment. Testing can measure ability but cannot predict success. Not only is testing limited in its capability to define a human's will, spirit, or desire, but tests are limited in scope. Psychological tests can be compared to laboratory tests. Although laboratory tests reveal important information, only a trained professional can apply that knowledge to form a diagnosis and then only by relying on all available data–not just a single fact, symptom, or test result. It is the social worker's responsibility to be fully prepared to use the data that a test suggests as only one piece of information in the puzzle to understanding an individual.

Do Not Testify Regarding Test Results if You Did Not Administer the Psychological Instrument

You may comment on your familiarity with the test in general, and on the testing done in the case at hand, but be clear that you are not the test giver and that you cannot interpret the results of any test that you have not personally administered. In testifying, you may state if you know whether the particular test has been scientifically studied for validity, reliability, and standardization, but nothing further. You should not present yourself as an expert on a particular test unless you have the necessary training, experience, and qualifications to do so.

If You Administer the Test, Know* As Much As Possible *About It

Social workers are frequently provided with information that includes psychological testing. Because judges and litigation attorneys are usually familiar with the major psychological tests such as the MMPI 1 and 2, social workers need to be familiar as well. Without at least a general knowledge of the parameters and meaning of the tests used, it is not possible to fully and accurately state an opinion about a client unless you have considered the information obtained from the test. This is especially true if testing results are contained in a client's file. This is not to say that social workers must test, but if testing is done on a client it is important that that piece of information forms part of the whole when called to testify. To ignore the tests result is, I believe, below the standard of care that is required of forensic social workers.

CONCLUSION

In general, people are interested in learning about themselves. Clients may thoroughly enjoy being part of the process in discovering their personal characteristics. Social workers will find that administering tests to clients can yield significant information about the client and contribute to the social worker's understanding of the client. Knowing that social workers are qualified to administer and score tests, testing can lead us into new and challenging areas of practice. Knowing as much as possible about the forensic setting will benefit your client and prepare you for the forensic setting.

Appendix A
Bylaws of the National Organization of Forensic Social Work

ARTICLE ONE

Definitions

As used in these Bylaws, the phrases, "social work and the law," "this area," and "the field" refer to those aspects of social work which involve close and significant contact with the law, such as crime and delinquency, competency, criminal responsibility, treatment of offenders, commitment procedures, social work aspects of marriage, divorce, annulment, and custody of children, personal injury and malpractice litigation, consultation to lawyers, worker's compensation, the civil rights of the mentally ill and mentally impaired, addiction to alcohol and drugs, social work testimony in court and before other bodies, confidentiality of records, etc. All definitions of other terms and words herein, unless applicable law otherwise requires, shall be as defined by the Bylaws, or by the Executive Council, in that order of precedence.

ARTICLE TWO

Name

The name of this organization shall be the NATIONAL ORGANIZATION OF FORENSIC SOCIAL WORK, hereinafter referred to as the "NOFSW."

ARTICLE THREE

Purpose

The NOFSW is organized and shall be operated exclusively for the primary purpose of education, as described in Section 501(c)(3) of the

---

Note: These bylaws are in committee for revisions.

Internal Revenue Code, or the corresponding section of any future federal tax code. Furthermore, the NOFSW is organized for scientific and charitable purposes as described in the aforementioned section.

The advancement of education in forensic social work in all its aspects encompasses, but is not limited to, the following specific objectives:

1. Organizing and implementing courses of instruction in the area of social work and the law, including training programs, forums, panels, and/or lectures for the purpose of improving and developing the capabilities of the membership.
2. The development of training programs for social workers desirous of increased skill and knowledge in the area of social work and the law.
3. Examining and certifying practitioners of forensic social work as to their competency in this field.
4. As a result of the educational pursuits of the NOFSW, the exchange of ideas and experience in those areas where social work and the law overlap, and the improvement of relationships between social workers and other professionals working in the field.
5. The dissemination of information to the public regarding the training, roles, and concerns of forensic social workers, and the potential contributions of the field.
6. The development of standards of practice in the relationship of social work and the law. Stimulating and encouraging scientific research in the field.
7. Publishing journals, newsletters, books or pamphlets, holding property, receiving grants and awards, monitoring research activities conducted under its auspices.
8. Making distributions to organizations that qualify as exempt organizations under section 501(c)(3) of the Internal Revenue Code.

ARTICLE FOUR

Powers

The NOFSW shall have the power, either alone or with others, to do any lawful act and to engage in any and all lawful activities which may be necessary, useful, desirable or proper for the furtherance of the purposes for which the NOFSW is organized, and to aid other organizations whose activities are such as to further or attain such purposes. Notwithstanding any other provision of these Bylaws, the NOFSW shall not carry on any other activities not permitted to be carried on by an organization exempt from Federal income tax under section 501(c)(3) of the Internal Revenue Code, or the corresponding section of any future federal tax code.

ARTICLE FIVE

Membership

1. *Eligibility.* Any person having reached the age of majority, holding American or Canadian citizenship and being of sound character with a professional interest in the practice of social work and the law will be eligible for membership in the NOFSW in one of its membership classes.
2. *Classes of Membership.* Membership shall consist of Founding Members, Full Members, Associate Members, Allied Professional Members, and Student Members. Under procedures developed by the Executive Council, after study by the Membership Committee, the NOFSW may create other classes of membership. Certification as Diplomate in Forensic Social Work shall be available only to Full members.
3. *Application for Membership.* An applicant for membership shall submit an application to the Chairperson of the Membership Committee for report and recommendation. An applicant whose credentials are in order shall be admitted to the appropriate class of membership.
4. *Voting Rights.* Each founding, full and associate member who is in good standing (with currently paid dues) shall have an equal vote in business of the NOFSW. All members shall have the right to speak to any issue but only those classes of members designated above shall have the right to vote.

ARTICLE SIX

Executive Council; Officers

1. *Executive Council.* The Executive Council shall consist of the President, the President-Elect, the Secretary, the Treasurer, the most recent living past President, and three (3) Council members elected at large.

2. *Elections and Terms of Office.* The following officers shall be elected by majority vote of a secret ballot of the membership in good standing of the NOFSW present at the Annual Meeting of the NOFSW: President-Elect, Secretary, Treasurer, and Councilors. The President-Elect and one Councilor shall be elected at each Annual Meeting. A Secretary and a Treasurer shall be elected at each alternate Annual Meeting. The President-Elect shall serve as such for one year as President for one year. A President-Elect shall not be eligible for re-election as President-Elect until one year after completing service as President. Councilors shall serve for three years with one Councilor elected each year. Candidates will be presented to the membership by the Nominating Committee at the Annual Meeting. Nominations, if seconded, can be received from the floor at the Annual Meeting. If there is more than one nominee for any office, election for that office will be by majority vote of a secret ballot of the membership of the NOFSW in good standing present. If there is only one nominee for an office, secret ballot need not be used.
3. *Duties of Officers*
   (a) *President:* The President shall be the chief executive officer of the NOFSW and, subject to the control of the Executive Council, shall in general supervise and control all of the business and affairs of the NOFSW. The President shall preside over all meetings of the membership or of the Executive Council at which he/she is present. The President shall also be a voting member of the Budget Committee, and shall be an ex-officio member of all other committees of the Executive Council. The President shall also perform all duties incident to the office of President and such other duties as may be prescribed by the Executive Council from time to time.
   (b) *President-Elect:* In the absence of the President, or in the event of his/her death, inability or refusal to act, the President-Elect shall perform the duties of the President, and when so acting, shall have all powers of and be subject to all the restrictions upon the President.
   (c) *Secretary:* The Secretary shall: (a) keep the minutes of the proceedings of the members and of the Executive Council in one or more books provided for that purpose; (b) see that all notices are duly given in accordance with the provisions of these Bylaws or as required by law; (c) be custodian of the corporate

records and of the seal of the NOFSW and see that the seal of the NOFSW is affixed to all documents the execution of which on behalf of the NOFSW under its seal is duly authorized; (d) keep a register of the post office address of each member which shall be furnished to the Secretary by such member; and (e) in general, perform all duties as from time to time may be assigned to him/her by the President or by the Executive Council.

(d) *Treasurer:* The Treasurer shall: (a) chair the Budget Committee; (b) have charge and custody of and be responsible for all funds and securities of the NOFSW; (c) receive and give receipts for moneys due and payable to the NOFSW in such banks, trust companies or other depositories as shall be selected by the Executive Council; and (d) in general perform all of the duties as from time to time may be assigned to him/her by the Executive Council or by the President. If required by the Executive Council the Treasurer shall give a bond for the faithful discharge of his/her duties in such sum and with such surety or sureties as the Executive Council may determine. The Treasurer shall provide a monthly accounting of the NOFSW's financial activity at each meeting of the Board of Directors and an annual accounting within 45 days of the end of each fiscal year.

4. *Executive Council Meetings.* Executive Council meetings will ordinarily be held in connection with the Annual Meeting of the NOFSW at a place and time designated by the President. Special meetings may be called by the President or by any three members of the Executive Council. At least seven days' notice of such a special Executive Council meeting shall be given to Executive Council members. When necessary, the Executive Council may transact its business by means of a conference telephone call or other means where all members can hear each other. The penultimate and the antepenultimate living Past Presidents will be notified of and will be invited to attend all meetings of the Executive Council, with floor privileges. Unless elected to office of the Council, only the most recent living Past President shall have the right to vote.
5. *Duties of the Executive Council.* The Executive Council will act for the NOFSW, speak in its name, have title to its property, and perform all acts necessary to achieve the purposes of the NOFSW, except when the membership is assembled in general meeting. On

those occasions, the general membership shall assume such powers.

6. *Temporary Filling of Office Vacancies.* If the position of President becomes vacant, the President-Elect will succeed to that title and office. If any other office or council position becomes vacant, the President, with the consent of the Executive council, will designate a member to finish the term. If any committee seat becomes vacant, the President then in office will name a member for the unexpired term.
7. *Presumption of Assent.* A member of the Executive Council who is present at a meeting of the Executive Council at which action on any corporate matter is taken shall be presumed to have assented to the action taken unless his/her dissent shall be entered in the minutes of the meeting or unless he/she shall file his/her written dissent to such action with the person acting as the Secretary of the meeting before the adjournment thereof or shall forward such dissent by registered mail to the Secretary of the NOFSW immediately after the adjournment of the meeting. Such right to dissent shall not apply to a member of the Executive Council.
8. *Conflict of Interest*
   (a) Any possible conflict of interest with respect to any issue on the part of any member of the Executive Council shall be disclosed to the other members prior to any discussion or action by the Executive Council or a committee thereof where the issue could become a matter of action. Disclosure may be made verbally to all Executive Council members or by way of an annual report of affiliations. A conflict of interest shall be made a matter of record.
   (b) Any Executive Council member who has a possible conflict of interest with respect to any matter shall neither vote nor exercise any personal influence in the disposition of such matter. The minutes of the meeting shall reflect the disclosure and such member's abstention from participation.
   (c) Although an Executive committee member with any possible conflict of interest shall not vote or exercise personal influence in the disposition of such a matter, the member shall report fully all pertinent knowledge about the matter and answer freely why a proposed decision or transaction could, or would not, be in the best interest of the NOFSW.

(d) The President may circulate annually to all Executive Council Members such questionnaires and other forms as may be necessary to further the policy of this section.

9. *Recall of Officers.* Recall of any elected officer may be initiated by a petition signed by thirty members in good standing or five percent of the membership, whichever is greater. A majority vote of members voting by special mail ballot shall effect recall.

ARTICLE SEVEN

Committees

1. *Standing Committees.* Standing Committees shall consist of the following:
   (a) A Program Committee shall be formed by the President. The President shall determine which member of this Committee shall be chairperson. The Program Committee will develop scientific and social programs on dates selected by the Executive Council and will be authorized to expend sums of money for that purpose within budgetary limits set by the Executive Council.
   (b) A Membership Committee shall be formed by the President. The President will select a chairperson. The Membership Committee will examine credentials of applicants for membership in the NOFSW and make recommendations thereon.
   (c) An Education Committee shall be appointed by the President. The President will select a chairperson. The Education Committee will assist in the development of educational programs at various training centers and in the establishment of study groups where formal training centers do not exist.
   (d) An Ethics Committee shall be formed by the President. The President will select a chairperson. The Ethics Committee will develop guidelines for ethical concerns of the NOFSW and will consider such questions of ethics that might be brought to its attention by the Executive Council. The Ethics Committee will sponsor such activities as to educate members about ethical standards and guidelines.
   (e) The Budget Committee shall consist of the President, the Treasurer, and the most recent Past President. The Treasurer will be the chairperson. The Budget Committee will formulate an op-

erating budget for the NOFSW and advise the Executive Council in financial matters.

(f) Other committees, including additional standing committees and ad hoc committees may be created by the Executive Council of the membership which, by its enabling resolution will indicate the size, term, mission, and authority of such committees.

2. *Committee Chairpersons.* All Chairpersons serve at the pleasure of the President. The Chairperson of each committee expires with the assumption of office by each new President.
3. *Committee Membership.* Any member, elected officer, or councilor may be appointed to or removed from a Committee by the President, and will serve at the pleasure of the Chairperson of that committee. When a vacancy occurs in any committee, the President will designate another member of the NOFSW to finish the unexpired portion of the term. Additional committee members may be appointed to any committee by the President at the request of the committee chairperson.

ARTICLE EIGHT

Meetings

1. *Annual Meeting.* The NOFSW shall hold at least one annual meeting each year at a place and time designated by the Executive Council. At each meeting, there will be a general membership business session and one or more professional programs. The regular election of officers shall take place only at the annual meeting.
2. *Other Meetings.* Other meetings may be held at a place and time designated by the Executive Council.
3. *Quorum.* A quorum for purposes of conducting general membership business will consist of ten members or ten percent of the membership whichever is greater. A quorum for the Executive Council will consist of at least four members which shall include the President.

ARTICLE NINE

Finances

Dues and Assessments. The expenses of the NOFSW will be met by dues and assessments distributed among the members and by income from various NOFSW revenue-producing activities. The Executive

Council will fix the amount of such dues or assessments. Dues of a student member shall not be set above fifty percent of dues of an associate member. A member in arrears in payment for one year shall be reported to the Executive Council. The Executive Council may waive payment of dues for sufficient reason or the member shall be suspended. Suspension from membership means that the member shall lose all benefits of membership but will continue to be listed as a member in the Membership Directory. After two years of such arrearage, the Executive Council may continue to waive payment of dues for sufficient reason or membership shall be terminated upon a majority vote of the Executive Council.

ARTICLE TEN

Contract, Loans, Checks, Deposits

1. *Contracts.* The Executive Council may authorize any officer or officers, agent or agents, to enter into any contract or executive and deliver any instrument in the name of and on behalf of the NOFSW, and such authority may be general or confined to specific instances.
2. *Loans.* No loans shall be contracted on behalf of the NOFSW and no evidences or indebtedness shall be issued in its name unless authorized by a resolution of the Executive Council. Such authority may be general or confined to specific instances.
3. *Checks, Drafts, etc.* All checks, drafts, or other orders for the payment of money, notes or other evidences of indebtedness issued in the name of the NOFSW shall be signed by at least one (1) officer or agent of the NOFSW and in such manner as shall from time to time be determined by resolution of the Executive Council.
4. *Deposits.* All funds of the NOFSW not otherwise employed shall be deposited from time to time to the credit of the NOFSW in such banks, trust companies, or other depositories as the Executive Council may select.

ARTICLE ELEVEN

Fiscal Year

The fiscal year of the Corporation shall begin on the first day of January and end on the last day of December of each year.

ARTICLE TWELVE

Corporate Seal

The Executive Council shall provide a corporate seal which shall be circular in form and shall have inscribed thereon the name of the NOFSW and the state of incorporation and the words "Corporate Seal."

ARTICLE THIRTEEN

Waiver of Notice

Unless otherwise provided by law, whenever any notice is required to be given to any member or executive councilperson of the NOFSW under provisions of these Bylaws or under the provisions of the Michigan Non-Profit Corporation Act, a waiver thereof in writing, signed by the person or persons entitled to such notice, whether before or after the time stated therein, shall be deemed equivalent to the giving of such notice.

ARTICLE FOURTEEN

Amendments

1. *Proposed Amendments by the Executive Council.* The Executive Council has the authority to submit any proposed amendments to these Bylaws to the membership at an annual meeting.
2. *Proposed Amendments by the Membership.* Any member may submit a proposed amendment by mail or at a general business meeting on written petition signed by at least twenty members or ten percent of the membership, whichever is less.
3. *Approval of Amendments.* In order to become effective, an amendment must be approved by two-thirds of the membership voting. A vote on a proposed amendment may be taken either by a mail ballot or if prior notice has been received, by the membership, at an Annual Meeting.

ARTICLE FIFTEEN

Parliamentary Authority

1. *Parliamentary Authority.* Unless otherwise provided in the Bylaws, the conduct of meetings of the Executive Council and of the membership shall be governed by rules promulgated by the Execu-

tive Council or, in the absence of such rules, by the rules contained in *Robert's Rules of Order, Newly Revised,* latest edition available.

2. *Suspension of Rules.* The rules promulgated by the Executive Council governing the conduct of meetings may be suspended at any meeting by a majority of the members present.

ARTICLE SIXTEEN

Earnings and Propaganda

No part of the net earnings of the NOFSW shall inure to the benefit of, or be distributable to its members, officers, or other private persons, except that the NOFSW shall be authorized and empowered to pay reasonable compensation for services rendered and to make payments and distributions in furtherance of the purposes set forth in Article Three hereof. No substantial part of the activities of the NOFSW shall be the carrying on of propaganda, or otherwise attempting to influence legislation, and the NOFSW shall not participate in, or intervene in (including the publishing or distribution of statements) any political campaign on behalf of or in opposition to any candidate for public office.

ARTICLE SEVENTEEN

Dissolution

Upon the dissolution of the NOFSW, no member or director shall be entitled to any distribution or division of its remaining assets, and after the payment of all debts and obligations of the NOFSW, the assets shall be distributed for one or more exempt purposes within the meaning of section 501(c)(3) of the Internal Revenue Code, or the corresponding section of any future federal tax code, or shall be distributed to the federal government, or to a state or local government, for a public purpose.

ARTICLE EIGHTEEN

Indemnification of Officer and Directors

To the extent allowed by law, the NOFSW shall be empowered to indemnify any and all persons who have served at any time as Executive council members or officers, or who, at the request of the Executive Council of the NOFSW may serve or at any time have served as directors or officers of another corporation in which the NOFSW at such time owned or may own shares of stock and their respective heirs, administrators, successors and assigns, against any and all expenses, including amounts paid upon judgments, counsel fees, and amounts paid in settlement (before or after suit is commenced), actually and necessarily incurred by such persons in connection with the defense or settlement of any claim, action, suit or proceeding in which they, or any of them, are made parties, or a party, or which they, by reason of being or having been directors or officers of the NOFSW, or of such other corporation, except in relation to matters as to which any such director or officers or persons shall be adjudged in any action, suit, or proceeding to be liable for his/her own negligence or misconduct in the performance of duty. Such indemnification shall be in addition to any other right to which those indemnified may be entitled under law, the NOFSW's Articles of Incorporation, these Bylaws, agreement, vote of directors, or otherwise.

IN WITNESS WHEREOF, for the purposes of forming this association, the undersigned have executed these Bylaws on this 6th day of September 1983.

____

Dane S. Hughes, AFSW

Amended May 1997

Amended May 1999

Appendix B

National Organization of Forensic Social Work Code of Ethics

PREAMBLE

In accepting membership in the National Organization of Forensic Social Work, each Forensic Social Work Practitioner solemnly pledges to adhere to the Code of Ethics. The Forensic Social Work Practitioner agrees, in accordance with this Code of Ethics, to fulfill the following obligations to society, fellow colleagues and their organizations, individual members of the National Organization of Forensic Social Work and the National Organization of Forensic Social Work. Each Forensic Social Work Practitioner shall promote well being, minimize potential harm, and encourage the equal availability of quality Forensic Social Work services to all.

Section I

Ethical Responsibility to the National Organization of Forensic Social Work

Canon 1. Each member of the National Organization of Forensic Social Work shall possess the required qualifications of education, background and experience to perform the duties of a Forensic Social Work Practitioner.

Canon 2. Members of the National Organization of Forensic Social Work shall not misrepresent a member's qualifications, education, background or experience either orally or in writing for any purpose, including purposes of obtaining membership, licensing and/or certification.

Note: These codes of ethics are in committee for revisions.

Canon 3. Each Forensic Social Work Practitioner shall keep abreast of changing laws affecting practice, participate in in-service training programs, attend professional conferences, expand their practice skills through professional publications, consult on forensic matters with professional colleagues, and present educational material to colleagues and other professionals when so requested.

Canon 4. Each member shall be responsible for informing other professionals and the public about the work and standards of the National Organization of Forensic Social Work.

Canon 5. The Forensic Social Work Practitioner shall clearly distinguish between his/her statements made on behalf of the National Organization of Forensic Social Work and those made as a private citizen.

Canon 6. The Forensic Social Work Practitioner shall attempt to clearly identify potential conflicts among laws, rules, policies and treatment goals when serving the client, in consultation with other agencies or with members of society.

Canon 7. Each Forensic Social Work Practitioner who pursues scholarly inquiry through research and publication shall insure confidentiality and minimize physical and/or psychological harm to all clients.

Canon 8. Members of the National Organization of Forensic Social Work shall only participate in research with subjects who have voluntarily given his/her informed written consent. Care shall be taken to protect the privacy and dignity of research subjects. There shall be no penalty to the client for refusal to participate in any research project.

Canon 9. Appropriate credit should be given in publications according to standards set by publishers. Major contributors shall be listed. The primary author should be listed first.

Section II

Ethical Responsibilities to Employers and Colleagues

Canon 10. The Forensic Social Work Practitioner shall adhere to commitments voluntarily entered into between the Forensic Social Work Practitioner and the employing agency.

Canon 11. The Forensic Social Work Practitioner shall report unethical conduct of employers or colleagues to appropriate agencies and/or professional organizations.

Canon 12. The Forensic Social Work Practitioner shall refuse to participate in any unethical conduct or procedure against any client, colleague or agency.

Canon 13. The Forensic Social Work Practitioner shall treat clients, colleagues, supervisees, students and trainees with respect and dignity.

Canon 14. The Forensic Social Work Practitioner shall conduct evaluations of supervisees, students or trainees in a fair and equitable manner according to agency norms or personnel practices. Such evaluations shall be shared with the subject of said evaluation.

Canon 15. The Forensic Social Work Practitioner shall consult with colleagues upon request.

Canon 16. The Forensic Social Work Practitioner shall not solicit clients from the member's agency for private practice unless such is in accordance with the agency's policies.

Section III

Ethical Responsibilities to Clients

Canon 17. The Forensic Social Work Practitioner shall not discriminate on the basis of race, nationality, religion, color, age, sex, sexual orientation, mental or physical disability, political belief, marital, or legal status in providing Forensic Social Work services.

Canon 18. The Forensic Social Work Practitioner shall clearly identify the source of referral, inform individuals being evaluated or treated of the nature and purpose of the evaluation, and use applicable standards of confidentiality with whom the information will be shared.

Canon 19. The Forensic Social Work Practitioner shall not provide treatment that could endanger the physical, emotional or psychiatric health of the client.

Canon 20. The Forensic Social Work Practitioner shall seek consultation when appropriate.

Canon 2l. The Forensic Social Work Practitioner shall make referrals to other professionals and agencies when it is deemed to be in the best interest of the client. The client shall be informed of such referral.

Canon 22. The Forensic Social Work Practitioner shall avoid potential conflicts of interest by refusing to accept clients when there is a possible conflict between personal, family and/or professional responsibilities.

Canon 23. When terminating treatment against the client's wishes, care shall be taken to adequately explain the basis for the Forensic Social Work Practitioner's decision and to insure the opportunity for continuity of services by appropriate referral to other professionals or agencies.

Canon 24. The Forensic Social Work Practitioner shall protect the confidentiality of all records and documents subject to law. Disclosures of information shall be made only with the client's informed, written consent.

Canon 25. The Forensic Social Work Practitioner shall set reasonable and customary fees, which are in accordance with rates for services performed of a similar nature by other professionals.

Canon 26. The Forensic Social Work Practitioner shall make services available to selected indigent clients.

Canon 27. The Forensic Social Work Practitioner shall receive remuneration for services performed.

Canon 28. The Forensic Social Work Practitioner shall not engage in any illegal activities, fraud or deceit.

Canon 29. The Forensic Social Work Practitioner shall not accept, demand, give or receive anything of value for making or receiving a referral from a colleague.

Canon 30. The Forensic Social Work Practitioner shall not allow his/her personal problems, mental illness, or drug or alcohol dependency to interfere in the delivery of services to clients. The Forensic Social Work Practitioner has the responsibility to seek appropriate treatment.

Canon 31. The Forensic Social Work Practitioner shall not engage in any sexual contact with clients, students, or any person under the authority of the Forensic Social Work Practitioner.

Canon 32. The Forensic Social Work Practitioner shall report any documented or suspected child abuse or neglect, abuse of patients or any other dependent persons to appropriate local or federal agencies in accordance with relevant local and national laws.

Canon 33. The Forensic Social Work Practitioner shall notify both the appropriate legal authorities and identified potential victim(s) when serious threats to do imminent bodily harm are made by clients.

Canon 34. The Forensic Social Work Practitioner shall obtain written consent of clients when video taping or recording interviews for professional or educational purposes.

Canon 35. The Forensic Social Work Practitioner shall be mindful of special duties to clients under legal age and shall insure that only the necessary information to maximize the client's progress in treatment be given to parents, guardians or appropriate agencies.

Section IV

Ethical Responsibility to Society

Canon 36. The Forensic Social Work Practitioner has an obligation to impact proposed legislation affecting the practice of Forensic Social Work.

Canon 37. The Forensic Social Work Practitioner shall promote quality services and high standards for Forensic Social Work care equally to all people.

Canon 38. The Forensic Social Work Practitioner shall not perjure him/herself.

Canon 39. The Forensic Social Work Practitioner shall not delegate duties or responsibilities to any person not qualified to perform those duties or to accept those responsibilities.

Canon 40. The Forensic Social Work Practitioner shall not use professional knowledge and skills in any enterprise detrimental to the public well being.

Revised at Annual Meeting: March 28, 1987

Index

Page numbers followed by the letter "f" indicate figures; those followed by the letter "t" indicate tables.